RED ARMY GENERAL

RED ARMY GENERAL

Leading Britain's Biggest Hooligan Firm

Tony O'Neill

MILO BOOKS

First published in November 2004 by Milo Books Ltd

This paperback edition first published June 2005

ISBN 1 903854 45 8

Typeset in Goudy by Avon DataSet Ltd,
Bidford on Avon, Warwickshire, B50 4JH

Printed and bound in Great Britain by
Cox & Wyman, Reading

MILO BOOKS LTD
The Old Weighbridge
Station Road
Wrea Green
Preston
PR4 2PH
info@milobooks.com

Contents

PROLOGUE

IF YOU'VE READ the jacket, you'll already know what this book's about. It is the story of two decades, the 1970s and most of the 1980s, that I spent following Manchester United. A life of dedication to my boyhood heroes, and a life of extraordinary violence and excitement off the pitch. It's also a story that cannot be fully told, because there are too many tales and too many secrets to be kept. What it is not is an attempt to glorify United's football firm by saying we battered everyone. I don't have to try to impress anyone. At the end of the day, everyone knows what we did. Our actions speak for themselves.

The modern-day Stone Island cyber-hooligan needs to understand something. The Seventies was our baby. We were children of the Red Army, the biggest mass following British football has ever seen and will ever see. We grew up steeped in rucking, robbing and wrecking. Whatever happens, happens: that was our philosophy. By the time the Eighties came around, the age of new, streamlined mobs, we had seen and done it all before. Nothing intimidated us. Other teams might quake and cave in at the reputation of one of the new mobs. Not us. We relished it.

The late Eighties, when Greater Manchester Police undertook a massive operation into United's firm, and the Nineties I have kept for a second and final book. There was too much to tell in one volume and, believe me, that stuff needs a book in its own right.

People have wanted me to write my story for several years, yet it's something I never intended to do. Until I was imprisoned for events around the England–Greece game a few years ago, the idea of a book broke all boundaries. I had never understood why someone would want to write a story that was essentially grassing on both himself and his friends. That was certainly not something I could do.

Then while I was inside, my solicitor Matthew Claughton, at Olliers in Manchester, was approached with an offer for me to write my tale, as the publisher believed I had a good story to tell. I thought about it and it occurred to me that if anyone at United was there all the way through, it was me. I had been at it for three decades, and there is hardly anyone else in our world who can or would say that. So I agreed. Hence this book was mainly prepared by me while enjoying the delights of Sudbury Open Prison, but completion was delayed because I was moved to Strangeways after some false allegations were made about me by a grass inside, and I had to wait until I was released in June 2004 before I could finish it. One thing I want to stress is that none of the names mentioned herein relate to anyone who, over the past ten to fifteen years, has gone to football matches and participated in violence.

I have had help from a few sources in putting this together, and I'd like to thank them, but most of it is based on my own recollections. I didn't keep a diary, so it has come from my head. So anyone who spots a date or a detail I've got wrong, or if I haven't always minded my P's and Q's, don't let it bother you. I guarantee the account will be correct in its essentials. Nothing in this book is made up. I don't consider myself an author; I'm certainly not an author of self-delusion, as seems to be the case with some.

A word on the title of this book, *Red Army General*. The police have alleged in court that I was the 'general' of United's hooligans. Now that is a word none of the lads would use about me or anyone else. Instead it's the sort of thing the police say in court because it makes you sound ten times worse than you are. It's a term they use to help get people convicted in the absence of any concrete evidence. So I decided to use it myself as a piss-take of them.

A lot of people have wished me well, but there are also one or two that friends and I have come into contact with who seem jealous and cannot bear to support me. All I can say to them is that throughout my life, jealousy has never been one of my characteristics. People have always asked things of me and I have always helped, something which has often been detrimental to my family life. For once I'm doing something for me, something that I hope also brings some enjoyment and food for thought to others.

I have been asked how I justify the things that we did. Well, why should I? My thing was smacking people in the face who wanted it. If they didn't want it, there was no problem. Football brought an excitement into our lives that we couldn't get anywhere else. If you wanted to escape a life of council estate drudgery, that's how it was. And truthfully I had a riot, regardless of certain stitches in my head and prison sentences. There are always one or two regrets, something you may have said to someone, but not to do with football. I have been round the world and nearly every country in Europe. I've had a life.

People have also asked me what Manchester United's main hooligan firm was called in the Seventies and Eighties. Well, we never needed a silly name. We were United.

CHAPTER ONE

WYTHENSHAWE REDS

I WAS BORN and raised on the biggest council estate in Western Europe.

Wythenshawe sprawls across a vast area of south Manchester. Cut off by the River Mersey from the city, its population of 150,000 live in nine wards stretching as far south as Manchester Airport and the edge of Cheshire commuter belt. It was designed as a 'garden suburb' – every house had a garden – with lots of trees and space. It might not have had the ugly high-rises that deformed a lot of inner-city areas but it was still a sink estate, where families were dumped and left without a lifeline. It took in overspill population from the city centre and a lot of the residents came originally from tough slums.

One thing they forgot to put in was anything for young people to do. The original bored teenager could have come from Wythenshawe, and it became a breeding ground for youth gangs. Each patch had its gang and some of them were very violent. The potential for trouble was always there. Gangs provided the excitement that, as a youngster, I craved, and from there it was a natural progression to the even bigger mobs of the terraces.

I was born in 1958, one of four brothers in a three-bedroom corner council house. My dad died when I was seven. He had been in the Army, then worked at Dunlop and got cancer from the black tar smoke from the tyres; there was little health and safety in those days. I watched my old lady bring up four lads and work herself into the ground – and when she needed help off the authorities, she never got it. In those days if the kids did anything wrong they were carted off to the children's home. My old lady was always desperate to keep us in check so we wouldn't be taken away, and her method of controlling us was to leather us.

Perhaps because my dad was dead, I grew up pretty fast. When I was ten, I asked myself, what is this all about? I've got fifty years' work ahead of me, and for what? To live like this? We had no luxuries. I looked at my mam, struggling like fuck. We always went to school clean but we were poor, no messing; I had my brother's shoes with holes in, always wore hand-me-downs – and we weren't the worst off by any means. My mam seemed to get no reward for working all hours and always faced that constant pressure that we might be dragged off for doing something wrong.

The area we lived in was called Crossacres. I went to the local junior school but was then sent by my mam to Poundswick Upper, a big comprehensive in Woodhouse Park. Everyone where I lived went to Sharston School but I had to travel all the way to Poundswick because that was where my mum sent us. I used to have all my Sharston pals waiting for me going to school to have fights with me just for fun. My schoolbooks would be scattered all over as we fought in the street. I only had one fight at school itself. This kid thought he was the cock and was gobby so I hit him one day and sorted his nose out for him. Me and my mate Dave Scanlon, who was a hard lad, were rated the handiest but we didn't have a fight to prove who was cock of the school because there was no sense to it.

I loved all sports. Football was my favourite, though I did enjoy rugby because it was violent – until it came on top when we played the 'posh' kids from Stockport Grammar and some big lump got properly on my case. Some of those middle-class rugger boys are monsters on the pitch and this guy ironed me out, no messing.

Wythenshawe was like a city in itself. We hung about at the local row of shops but it was always a bit tricky because the cop shop was next door and the coppers were always on the beat and knew who was who. We didn't graffiti or vandalise – it wasn't the done thing. If you did that you were damaging your own, plus we knew all the shopkeepers and everyone was dead friendly.

Like I say, round our way it was all gangs. The Benchill Mob were probably the worst. They were always fighting the Baguley Boys, another tough crew, and that escalated to the point where they were throwing petrol bombs at each other. Baguley were also always having a go with the Woodhouse Park lads. My home in Crossacres was on the outskirts of the worst of the gang territories, though we sometimes fought with the Peel Hall lads. We were just happy-daft, not violent like the older Benchill lot – they were mental, vicious. Outsiders despised Benchill because it was classed as one of the poorest areas, and even today it has some of the worst deprivation and lowest income levels in the country.

You would get inter-school fights, and then rows between the different boys' clubs. Wythenshawe Park was always dodgy, an ambush place, especially when the funfair was in town. You always knew someone would get a good hiding – some people went in gangs thinking they were safe and would still get battered. I have had to get away from there a few times when it was proper dodgy. Whoever occupied the waltzers was the biggest mob. You would get the older ones, in their late teens, who would terrorise the rest. That's the way it was; you didn't question it.

*   *   *

IN MAY 1968, Manchester United defeated Benfica to win the European Cup. Like millions of others, I watched their triumph on a black and white telly, and it was fabulous. Everyone at school and in the streets was talking about it. The players seemed to have a glamour that no other team possessed, even the unheralded John Aston, the star of the final, a winger I loved for the way he jinked in and out and went on his runs.

I started going to matches at both Old Trafford and Maine Road the following season, when I was ten. A lot of people in those days would watch whichever Manchester team was at home, as away travel was not common. I never found the atmosphere as good at Maine Road, though they had a very good team themselves in that era.

Once I was on the big-match wavelength, I couldn't do without it: the roar of the crowds and the way they moved as one was an unbelievable buzz. On the terraces you could see the blokes with their new skinhead haircuts and steel-toecap boots, winding each other up, waiting for someone to start up the others and go into battle with someone, anyone. It didn't matter who it was, it was match day and it was fight time.

It wasn't just Wythenshawe that was gang-oriented. I soon found out that across the whole of Manchester, gang warfare was the 'in' thing. Wythenshawe, Salford, Collyhurst, Middleton, Gorton, Ardwick – whichever area you were from there were rivalries, and the terraces were where you could sort them out. Fortunately for all these thugs and criminals, something was stirring, something that would give them common cause and a new enemy to fight – the away fan.

The closest I came to being a terrace victim in my early match-going days was when stood in the Kippax Street end at Maine Road, at the age of twelve or thirteen. They were playing West Ham, and a very handy firm of East End boot boys had made the trip. Some of them, dressed in big white pants and enormous boots, appeared on the City terraces. They looked mean and really wanted it. Thirty or forty of these warriors emerged at about half past one from one side of the Kippax and came over a wall into the terracing, to an area where all the really hard City lads were supposed to stand. If I can see them, I thought, then surely the City fans can, but these blokes didn't seem to care. In my naivety, I was confused. Surely they didn't want to be seen by the City? Wouldn't they get battered? Weren't they scared?

Unbeknown to me, the rules of terrace warfare had changed. It was no longer enough to parade at a game in your colours; the visiting nutters had to prove themselves by going in, or trying to 'take', the away end. The West Ham moved across the Kippax from the back. Someone must have given the signal to attack and they swept down into the fans in front of them. City were slow to respond, not comprehending where the blows were coming from. West Ham swiftly dished it out to the nearest City fans, then regrouped, shouting and screaming hatred. With the initial shock over, they stood in the open, proud, defiant, victorious.

Now was the time for the City to react. Forward they surged, seeking revenge and willing each other on. West Ham had no choice but to go backwards and spread out, their organisation crumbling as the scale of their predicament became apparent. A beating looked inevitable.

Then, from my position of safety, I saw a big West Ham fan stride forward. From inside his coat he pulled an axe. As clear as day he held it aloft, waving it from side to side and beckoning the City with his other hand. My mouth fell open. This was not what it was all about – this was a nutter. I was transfixed, scared yet fascinated. He stood there, his face twisted into a snarl of hatred, brandishing this fearsome weapon and daring the City boys to do their worst. Naturally enough, the City fans stood back; not one fancied being the first in against this psychopath. Then as quickly as the West Ham had come they were gone, leaving a few sore heads and shocked expressions behind.

How could this happen in City's own end? Granted it was only half full at that time of the day, but I couldn't imagine anyone taking a liberty like that at Old Trafford. And so gradually United became the sole object of my support. I wanted to be with the mob that other fans were terrified of, not on the receiving end.

But I was still only a boy, still one of the pack of youngsters who would stand outside the ground at end of the game waiting to get autographs. You soon sorted out your favourites from the rest. Bobby Charlton was a Red legend but he was always dismissive towards us and I haven't liked him since. You can imagine us kids from Wythenshawe, scarves waving, hanging around in the pitch black, missed the bus but it didn't matter, we were there for our heroes – and he just dismissed us. We would also stand outside The Avenue in Mersey Bank, where George Best stayed, and wait to see if his car went past. I once stood there for ages and his car came round the corner. 'There he is!' someone shouted, but we didn't even wave, just watched him go past. Best to us was like a god because of all the publicity, the first pop star footballer in the world.

I was always independent. I was going to the match without an adult, and was in and out of the Benchill pub when I was twelve. I would rush home on match days to flog the *Manchester Evening News* sports supplement, *The Pink*, which was a big seller in those days, and had many a fight outside the pub with other lads who wanted to sell there. I also got boxing lessons from the bloke around the corner, Mr Lyons. He was the trainer for his son, who was a proper fighter. He taught me how to put up my fists and properly throw a punch, and he wouldn't mess about – he would really give me some digs. I would go home with a fat lip or my eyes discoloured, but it toughened me up – not that it needed it, as I've always been able to have a fight.

Anyway, you don't have to be a tough nut to be a football hooligan. It's not about toughness. I have known blokes as hard as nails who couldn't hack football violence because it is not a controlled situation. They couldn't handle the environment. They turned up with their pals and crapped it and kept at the back. Some of these same blokes could beat me up in a one-on-one, these steroid heads who think they are doormen, but they can't handle the violence in a football arena. They don't understand it because they weren't brought up with it. To them it is mayhem and chaos but I understand it and can deal with it quickly. I know what is going to happen, what is coming. But then I wouldn't understand being a doorman. I wouldn't know how to react. Boxers react in their ways, doormen in theirs, and football hooligans in theirs.

The first time I saw trouble at Old Trafford was against West Brom. I was standing in the old Scoreboard End, barely big enough to see over the heads in front of me, and I think we lost 2-1. Fewer than 200 West Brom fans stood huddled together at the top of the Scoreboard End and I found it weird at first that nothing was happening, because to me gangs were gangs and you had a fight. I was fascinated by people who didn't live in Manchester. To me they were the enemy but they looked straight members, they weren't a gang of hooligans. They didn't look as though they wanted trouble, but there was no segregation in the ground, one thing led to another, and eventually they got slapped.

By the time I decided United were my team, I had seen violence at both Manchester grounds and loved watching, willing on the frenzied, flailing crowd, with everybody roaring and running and the police frantically fighting to restore order. To me it was amazing. When you're young you search for stimulation, and football was the only thing available to me. Eventually I started going with my own little group of mates from the estate, our ages ranging from thirteen to seventeen, and that became our gang. I soon took control. I was the more dedicated follower of United and because I wandered freely over the estate I knew more people than my pals.

Old Trafford was different to Maine Road. Lads would be outside on the prowl, watching and waiting for the scarf boys with wrists enveloped with their club colours, something which was a must if you thought you were a hard nut. The away fan had to show his colours to prove he had been, but at Old Trafford that was likely to have only one outcome. Never mind if you managed to get in the old Scoreboard End, you were spotted by the hordes inside and it would not take long before you were surrounded. Then you saw the panic set in. In the end away fans had stopped coming because it was so dangerous. Old Trafford became a no-go area.

* * *

SOME SAY THE Red Army was born on a famous trip to West Ham in 1967, our last away game of that title-winning season. They had three World Cup winners in their side – Moore, Hurst and Peters – and had won the European Cup Winners Cup in 1965, but we destroyed them 6–1 to win the championship. And on the terraces we showed the East End what football support was all about: thousands of United swamped the ground, 500 occupied the North Bank, twenty fans ended up in hospital and the feared Hammers were humiliated, something they would never forget.

I wasn't there – I was only nine – but from then on United regularly had massive away support. Attendances both home and away rose even higher after the European Cup win as United became the most glamorous club in the country. It also meant others, jealous of our success and our support, were looking out for us, and it wasn't long before all those fans attracted bad headlines. Train-wrecking and mass brawls became the order of the day. At many grounds you could walk all the way around the terraces without any segregation, and fans would sometimes swap ends at half-time. It was a recipe for aggro.

Certain London clubs, particularly Millwall, held bad reputations for crowd disorder, but in the Sixties the biggest fights were between the giant northern clubs. People forget how much the North dominated football then. Between 1963 and 1970, the league champions were Everton, Liverpool, Man United, Liverpool, Man United, Man City, Leeds and Everton, in that order. London and the Midlands didn't get a look in. Bitter rivalries were forged in that Busby-Shankly-Mercer-Revie era that would persist for the next thirty years.

When people talk about the start of modern-day, post-1966 football hooliganism, they ought to look to Merseyside. Their fans terrorised visitors all through the decade. They were more ruthless, more merciless than anyone else. They would threaten you with knives and steal your money and even your clothes. Going there was like nowhere else, and when both Liverpool and Everton started to travel in big numbers too, they took that attitude with them. A lot of United fans came a cropper against these vicious bastards, and it wasn't long before we decided to do something about it.

One of the toughest United crews to emerge came from the Collyhurst and Miles Platting area of north Manchester. These were real inner-city tykes and they were not going to take the Scousers' shit lying down. One of their main faces was George Lyons, whose nickname was 'Mad Eyes'.

George Lyons: *I was born in 1951 and started watching United in 1964–5. Gibbo from Wythenshawe was the main lad at Man United then. He was a big lad, fat but big. We had our own young Collyhurst crew but when you are sixteen you look up to these guys.*

It all started with Liverpool and Everton. My first away

match was Liverpool in November 1967. They had just won the league. We went on a coach but I didn't have a ticket and couldn't get in the ground. I stood outside till about twenty minutes to go, when this side door opened and a St John Ambulance bloke came out with a lad I knew, who'd been beaten up inside. I stood with him and this St John Ambulance bloke said, 'Have you just come out of the ground?'

'Yeah,' I said. 'I came out to look after him.'

'Well, you'd better get back in there, catch the end of the game.'

So he took me in. I went up these stairs onto the terraces. United had a corner and it came over and Best scored. I jumped up to celebrate, as you do, and this big docker threw me down the stairs and nearly broke my ribs. That was my introduction to football violence.

United won 2–1, I think Best got both. We came out of the ground and it was going off all over. Eventually we made it back to the coach and a lad said, 'You'd better get down.'

I said, 'Why?' Next minute, all the windows went in.

Every time we went to Liverpool or Everton after that, it was always fighting. We got beat up at Everton one match coming back to Lime Street, down Scotty Road. My mate got his nose broken, I got a brick on me head, and a couple of lads got their coats taken off them.

I was getting a bit fed up of it, going to the matches and getting chased, so when they came to Old Trafford we got a big crew together, thirty or forty of us at first. We turned the tables and gave it to them, attacking them and putting the windows in on their coaches.

We played Everton in the League Cup. We spotted about four of them. One had a sheepskin on, so I thought, I'm going to have that. I came out of the ground, gave him a smack and pulled his coat off his back. His keys fell out of the pocket.

He said, 'You can have my sheepie, just give me my keys back.'

I said, 'Fucking swim for that, you Scouse bastard,' and threw them in the Manchester Ship Canal. They'd done so much to us in the past that there was no way we'd give them a break.

We played Everton again the season after and we followed a couple of them over to Salford way, gave them a couple of digs and one of them pulled out a knife. So my mate battered him and then the Scouser's dad came – he must have come in the car with his old feller.

His dad said, 'Don't you think you're a bit old to be hooligans?'

So my mate said, 'No. My dad's waiting down the road with his dad and even he'll throw a few bricks at you, you Scouse twats.'

It always seemed to be a night match when we played Everton. Our plan was always safety in numbers and stick together, but I still got my head kicked in a few times. Then we started waiting for them to come to Manchester. It wasn't good when I think about it now. I wanted to watch United. It was more a game then because I could run if I needed to. My bottle went sometimes and I did used to run.

There are stories that on one occasion in the mid-Sixties, Everton became the only mob ever to take the Stretford End. I don't know if that's true but the Scousers did seem to be as much up for the aggro as the football. The only away fans I saw in a proper mob in Manchester up to my mid-teens was eighty or ninety Liverpool vermin. Vermin is the word I use for them because of the atrocities they have committed with their knives and Stanley blades. In all my time they have never changed: no blades, no fight. You see them in a mob always looking behind, shitting it.

I caught sight of this crew moving fast up Warwick Road and away. They were skinheads and boot boys, horrible-looking cunts. I couldn't understand where our mob was and why they weren't getting done in. I followed, watching their style. This was a firm in the street trying to survive, trying to get back home, a task I hadn't thought about until then, as I was not yet a seasoned traveller. Some of them whacked people in bus stops, kicked cars and smashed windows. I felt sick as I saw ordinary United fans getting punched and couldn't do anything about it. Where were the lads when they were needed? I eventually stopped following them, as it seemed they knew which way they were going and even at that young age I knew I could end up with a slapping. So I left to contemplate my next move. There must be more to this, I thought. It was about time I explored the away game – and Spurs was next.

CHAPTER TWO

THE HITCHHIKERS' GUIDE TO AGGRO

LONDON IS A long way away when you're a kid and there's nothing in your pocket, so I turned to older lads for advice. They suggested hitchhiking, and that's how I ended up on a Friday night on the M6, hitching a lift with my mate Steve Hesford. Steve is one of the straightest lads I know but what a barmpot. He couldn't fight but he would cause trouble anywhere and was funny as hell. Our aim was to get to Euston railway station, as we were told that many United lads would be waiting there for the special train from Manchester to come in, then they would all move on together to White Hart Lane.

We eventually managed to get lifts all the way down and were at Euston for early morning. We begged and stole for our breakfast and some ale money for later on and took in the surroundings: all around us were lads with scarves round their waists, wrists and foreheads, brooding and drinking, waiting till the Mancs got in.

The special train was due at about 12.30 and everyone was looking at the platform. Just before arrival there must have been 2,000 fans in and around Euston and you could feel the excitement building. The tension got stronger by the minute.

Then we heard the chant.

'United! United!'

Within seconds, it was deafening. Off they came, even before the train had stopped, jumping from the steps and tearing down the platform, screaming the name of United. Wave after wave poured off. The waiting police were simply brushed aside as the horde came running out of the station and charged down Euston Road towards Kings Cross. This was the Red Army in full flight, smashing anything in sight. All they wanted was violence – and I wanted it as well. I knew at that moment I could do whatever I wanted when I was with this mob. I had found the purpose I wanted and needed in life: a team to follow and a load of blokes who treated me as one of their own. I knew I had found my role – to be there in front of the lads, getting the buzz and hopefully, one day, taking on the role of leader. My fledgling gang was too small and not violent enough for me – I needed more.

The day didn't go as I expected. The trend at the time was to go into the opposition's end, but first Hesford and I had to get some cash. At the ground we went mooching about, leaving the cover of the Red Army. Once we'd got some coin we went in, heading, as we thought we should, for Tottenham's end and the second tier known as the Shelf. Unbeknown to us, this part of the ground had a fierce reputation – and we soon found out why.

There seemed to be a mood of excitement among the people milling on and around the stairs. We quickly made our way up to the top, which brought me to a halt. The place was heaving with big blokes. What do we do now? Where do we go? I was conscious not to reveal my accent, as despite my youth I was tall and my height could make me a target. Trying to explain my age while being kicked all over didn't appeal.

While debating what to do, it happened. All round us the roar of the crowd intensified and the terrace came alive, as if buffalo were trampling over ground. Gaps appeared despite the crush and we could see raised fists crashing down. Kicks started flying and people were being dragged to the floor. It was brutal – and it seemed to go on and on.

Here I was, my first away match, and it was all happening in front of me. I didn't have time to be scared but knew instantly where I was going – in the same direction as the lads dropping over the side and scrambling into the safety of United's end. The United lads had gone in the Shelf, shown and had a go but knew they were never going to be able to stand their ground. It was all part of the fun.

After the game, we came out into a war zone. There was no police escort or controlled movement out, we just spilled into the street to be confronted by thousands of wild-eyed Cockneys. This was now the challenge: stick with the mob and get back to Euston alive. Time after time, mass brawls broke out, with the odd few coppers wading in with their truncheons, smacking anyone. It didn't matter to them, they were enjoying it. Seven Sisters Road was a long walk that day. More than a few became casualties but they had done a job, stuck together and given as good as they got.

Euston Station was like a fort held by troops desperate to stop the enemy overrunning their positions. Several times hundreds of United fans charged through the doors to stop Spurs trying to pick off stragglers. Soon the Army was in charge and for ninety minutes they roamed about, legging groups of Cockneys away from the station.

It was time to reflect what had gone on as I made my way home after sneaking on the train. There were probably a couple of hundred others who didn't pay either, something which many of us would continue to do in the years to some. It had been a long and draining day but what excitement and what an unbelievable experience, something I couldn't wait to recommend to my pals back home. I had found my mark in life and I wanted more. By Christ, I made sure I got it.

* * *

AFTER HEARING MY eventful tales of Spurs away, the rest of my little gang were soon keen to travel to watch United. I used to wander all the areas in Wythenshawe – Benchill, Woodhouse Park, Newall Green, Peel Hall, the lot – and knew loads of lads my age and older. None of us had any money, so the regular hitchhiking began. I don't know what our parents were thinking of, as most of us were in our early teens, but no-one stopped us.

Our first journey together took us to Wolverhampton in August 1971. All summer seemed to build up to the game – we were like kids anticipating Christmas. The plan was simple, mainly because we didn't have a clue. We met on the Friday night. Those who could afford them wore Dr Martens (I was never a skinhead because I couldn't afford a Crombie) and we all had scarves around our wrists. We thought we were the bee's knees, especially as everyone was drinking cider and bitter, which made us think we were even harder. The funny thing was, as a gang we hadn't done any real fighting together, so we didn't know who were the fighters and who were the talkers. We would soon find out.

We took a local train – without paying – to Knutsford in Cheshire and then walked to the nearby service station on the M6 motorway. It was ten o'clock and we split up into threes and fours to get rides, with the route in mind and a meeting place set for the next day. Then followed hours of chaos: everyone was fucking about, all running over when any car or wagon pulled up, arguments and the odd punches being thrown as we tried to pinch each other's lifts, but by two o'clock in the morning, and quite sober and cold, I was on my way.

If anyone reading this ever goes down the M6 and comes to the A49 turnoff for Wolverhampton, you'll see a field on your right. Thirty years ago there was a barn in the middle of that field and that's where at least fifteen of us spent the night trying to keep warm. What had started out as a gang, clean and eager, was now a scruffy, smelly bunch of council estate bums. But the sign at the roundabout as the sun came up said 'Wolverhampton' and our spirits lifted. We all soon found lifts and met up again in the town near a church, which became our base for an hour or two. More Reds joined us in dribs and drabs. We lay down on the grass banking, sunbathing and waiting for the Army to arrive.

From nowhere, a crew of Wolves were spread out across the street, screaming in our direction. They were right on us, in our faces. There was no time to organise the gang, no time to even think. I knew instinctively that I had to act. I jumped up and ran at them, my scarf flying around my neck. What happened next was my first step on the dangerous, rocky road to becoming a mob leader – a Red Army General.

The rest of the lads charged with me.

There were about seventy of us and only about forty Wolves but we were mostly inexperienced kids. Still, everyone screamed at the top of our voices and Wolves backed away. We hit them near some bus shelters and the punches flew in. It was fantastic. Pure adrenalin coursed through our limbs as the lads launched into these older blokes. We didn't care; we had watched before when one mob ran at another and we knew the more hesitant group would fold. We had to be decisive.

Some of the Wolves did stand and fight but we were flying all around them. I set my sights on the biggest lad at the front and punched him on the side of the head. He stumbled and bounced off the bus shelter back towards me. He was about to swipe me with a cosh when Dave Walker joined me and stuck an almighty boot in his side, swiftly followed by a blow to the head. The big lad scrambled away and was on his toes with the rest of them, being chased by more Reds.

We had won our first gang fight. The lads had shown they were up for it and had not let each other down. I'm sure we'd have stuck together even if they'd legged us – something that would happen more than once in the future, I don't mind admitting – but this moment was ours, and the day was only just beginning.

One thing it did alert us to was that this was a big day for Wolves as well. They too had been waiting all summer for the Red Army to arrive and were going to do their best to stop it from reaching the ground, if they could. The town began to get lively, with little outbreaks of fighting, especially once the pubs opened. We couldn't enjoy a beer as we didn't have a bean between us, so we hung around near the train station, meeting people and letting them know what had gone on and who was where.

High noon brought it home to me that this was no picnic. I saw a pub up the high street explode. Both sets of fans had gone into this main boozer to try to hold an advantage and within half an hour it was half United and half Wolves. This was the start of the main event, with both sets of supporters smashing chairs and tables over each other. The noise from the windows going all over the road and the intense roar of battle soon brought everyone together. The main road looked like a scene from a Western, with everyone scrapping it out and the police diving in to try to stop the madness.

Soon there were that many Wolves thugs out for our blood that one half of town became a no-go area for Reds – and it was the half we'd have to go through to reach the ground. Not to worry: we knew the first of five special trains from Manchester was due in at 12.30 and the worst lunatics would be on that first one. All we could do was wait, as the city centre was no longer safe for our little gang.

When you know the train is due in there is a sense of excitement and pride. You know that hundreds are going to come bursting through, hellbent on destruction. The trouble is, the opposition would always check out the time of the Manc

18

train too, so it could be very dodgy hanging around waiting for it.

One minute before the train arrived, the Wolves charged down towards us again. There were probably 2–300 Reds in and around the station. Our gang stood together – Dave and Willie Farrell, the Prescott twins (John and Jimmy), Hesford, Walker and others. Wolves were getting through the police and we traded punches. These were no mugs, they were big blokes who knew how to fight and had seen it all before. We were so busy fending them off that we didn't hear the special arrive.

Just as it seemed we were losing, out of the station they came: the Red Army in full flow, running as fast as they could. Imagine it: 6–700 lads, all wanting aggro, all wearing the Seventies thug look: white half-mast pants so you could see their cherry red Doc Marten boots, with anything from eighteen to twenty-three lace holes; butchers' coats or Levi jackets worn skin tight and high up so the traditional Ben Sherman shirt could be seen; red and white scarves, or tartan, made fashionable by Rod Stewart. What a sight.

Wolves had put on a good show but now scattered through side streets and down roads. Casualties had been taken on both sides but United were in control of the city centre. We joined in, with everyone smashing windows. The noise of a shop front collapsing would never fail to get to me – it signalled to the opposition that we were on their territory and we'd done them. I know it sounds mad but when you're young, daft things make you happy.

The Red Army soon filled the pubs, leaving us to wander the streets. We still weren't proper drinkers yet, though that would change within a few months. The special trains continued to unload their hooligan cargo at regular intervals so we had no more worries on the streets, but it soon came to two o'clock, time to move off into enemy territory to get to the ground. I had to find more Reds I knew from Wythenshawe, lads who I knew were game for a fight – these were older lads and had a good reputation, as barmy as anyone.

If we were to find them it would be in a pub, and it didn't take us long. Here were some of the most notorious lads of their generation. You had Steve and Ray Gillham, who were twins and as big a pair of bastards at the match as you were ever likely to see. Whatever one did the other had to better, and usually succeeded. Then there was Mick and Paddy Ginty, who loved nothing better than getting pissed and throwing the odd table through a pub window; Pubby, who could talk your head off and always objected to whatever went on but would always be there; Mick Madden, who had evil eyes and whose party trick in a brawl was to smash his pint pot over your head; big Gibbo, who always acted like your dad, telling you how naughty you all were; Eric Hamnett, ever ready and always on the alert for the kick-off; and Spenner and Jack Barton, both big lads who could fight.

But one man stood out even in this crowd, a man everybody knew. He didn't give a toss who you were or where he was; if there was trouble, he would be first in. Jeff Lewis was already a legend. United fans up and down the country knew him as a fearless, raging bull. His long thick ginger hair and chunky frame were a familiar sight in the streets and on the terraces, and he wore his scarf around his neck with pride. Jeff was the main man, and had a hard, loyal following.

He would either start it, join in or finish it, it didn't matter to Jeff. He didn't think about it. He could drink and he could fight – and so could his wife. One night in the Benchill, a pub on the estate with a wild reputation, some bloke got into an argument with Mrs Lewis and stuck the nut on her. Nobody blinked when she came out with the classic line, 'No one butts me, not even my husband,' and proceeded to smash the bloke all over the room. Jeff, who remained propped at the bar, simply muttered, 'Leave it, it's not worth the trouble.' Pure class.

Having found the main Wythenshawe mob, we waited for them to leave. I knew that there was going to be trouble and lots of it, as the talk all day was that it would get worse around the ground. Some people kept going on about a subway you had to walk through. It meant nothing to me, but I was soon to find out about that subway, and so was my little gang.

The pub emptied and 250 people were on the march, with the Wythenshawe mob in full cry at the front. But something was nagging me about this ground and the impending fight; for once no one had mentioned going in their end. There was no police escort, and caution seemed to be the word. The nearer we got to the ground, the more crowded the streets became, with fans mingling together.

United were still singing and ready for it, but when it came it was a shock. I didn't realise as we descended a walkway that it led to the subway people had mentioned. Everyone was suddenly aware that it was on us, as blokes with different dress sense and accents were all around in this tight space. One man with enormous sideburns and frizzy hair started screaming and throwing punches in all directions. Then it became a free-for-all.

There were people lying on the floor getting a kicking, people standing toe to toe trading kicks and punches, you were fighting someone in front of you and taking whacks from behind   and all the time fear kept you on your feet. This was a proper set-to with both sets of fans giving it to each other: pure violence, proper adrenalin, sheer excitement, the real buzz. On it went in the subway, people shrieking and yelling, not knowing who you were hitting or who was hitting you. All you could do was try to stay with your pals and hope you got out the other end in one piece. This wasn't Wolves doing United or United doing Wolves, this was purely and simply people fighting because they loved it and didn't give a fuck about police – who were a joke anyway. Nothing mattered, not even getting hurt; this was Saturday, match day, and you had to fight – that's what it was all about.

The brawl ended as we spilled out of the subway into the daylight: United fans moved to their left and Wolves carried straight on. My pals and I were battered, bruised and shaken, but we were still together and laughing at each other as the shock wore off. I cannot explain how wonderful we felt – but we knew that more was needed.

United grouped on a corner, hundreds bouncing up and down screaming, 'Kill the bastards!' Then they surged down the side of the ground, knocking everyone and everything to the floor. We were rampaging, nothing was stopping us – or so I thought. But Wolves were no mugs. They were there all right. As we got halfway they were piling round from their end to meet the Red Army's advance. When I look back it's clear to me that United were saying, 'Yeah, okay, we can't get in your end but we'll put on a show to let you know we tried.' And the Wolves were ready and waiting to show United, 'You've no chance of taking our end, we'll kick your heads in.'

The police were whacking people from both groups over the head. It was like a game being played out by everyone and people knew what to expect: no arrests, just cut heads, nosebleeds and big lumps. The police had waited for the charge, letting the fighting start before pouring in themselves. It was great for all sides; no one cared, least of all the police, who seemed to be enjoying themselves and only nicked the ones who couldn't get off the floor because they had been smashed in and needed hospital treatment. Now I knew why no one had mentioned going in the home end: these Wolves were staunch. They loved it as much as United and they could give it out.

The game flashed by but that didn't matter. Our priority was getting home without any dosh. We were going to sneak on one of the special trains back to Manchester. Well, the word sneak is not strictly accurate because it didn't matter if you had no ticket, not with a couple of thousand barmy United fans on the platform and the police wanting to get you out of their town and restore order as quickly as possible. Our return through the city centre was muted considering how many hooligans there were. Some more shop windows went in but nothing like I expected. In fact it was a bit of a letdown for me. Some people would have sampled enough for one day but I had tasted football thuggery and wanted more and more. My appetite was insatiable. The buzz got me – and the buzz is an illness. Once it gets you it is always there, no matter what. I couldn't wait for the days to pass until the next match.

* * *

FANS BY NOW had adopted their own 'ends', where the main singers, fighters and characters liked to congregate. There was the Kop at Liverpool, the Shed at Chelsea, the North Bank at Arsenal, the Holte End at Villa, and so on. The Stretford End, that huge expanse of terracing behind one of the Old Trafford goals, was our focal point. It quickly became the most notorious end in football. Grown-ups would warn, 'Don't go on the Stretford End', but I was too independent to be told. I was a traveller and wanted to learn about things myself. We would queue up at twelve o'clock for a 3pm kick-off and there would be thousands waiting. If you weren't out of town and heading to the ground by 1.30 you wouldn't get in.

Lads naturally congregated in crews from their home areas and each had their own patch on the Strettie. Salford, for example, always occupied the area to the right of the entrance tunnel. Soon all the crew knew each other – and they didn't always get on. Inter-gang rivalry was a fact of life. On the estates around Manchester, lads from one youth club would attack the youth club across the street. If you were old enough, you had a pub as your base. People weren't running around in taxis everywhere in those days, they tended to socialise in their own locality. Life was tribal and territorial.

That meant that personal feuds could escalate. Say the Gillhams had trouble with a couple of lads from Salford; next thing that would blow up into a full Wythenshawe versus Salford confrontation. They would attack each other in the end itself or in the drinks stand underneath.

The Collyhurst lads were involved in one of these feuds:

> George Lyons: *I went to see a concert at Salford University. I went in this pub, the Woolpack, and a lad came up and asked where I was from.*
>
> *I said, 'Collyhurst, why?'*
>
> *He said I had five minutes to get out of the pub. I ended up getting chased through the streets of Salford by him and about twenty of his mates.*
>
> *The following Saturday, I was in the Scoreboard Paddock, where we made our name, and was telling all the lads what had happened to me when at that very minute the lad from Salford came and stood next to me. It was pure coincidence but I wasn't going to let it pass.*
>
> *I tapped him on the shoulder and said, 'All right?'*
>
> *He looked at me, a bit confused, and said, 'Yeah, why?'*
>
> *I smacked him and he went down. Then we battered him and his mates. The coppers looked at us as if we had two heads. They came in and asked what was going on and I told them, 'We just had a bit of an argument.' They thought we were acting the goat.*
>
> *That was when I got to know O'Neill and all that lot because the Wythenshawe crowd were leaning towards backing Salford, but in the end we all came together.*

Before and during a game you would hear endless rival chants:
'Middy, Middy, Middleton.'
'Shit!'
'Withy, Withy, Wythenshawe.'
'Shit!'
'Salford. Salford.'
'Oh Collyhurst, is wonderful, oh Collyhurst is wonderful . . .'
Then everyone would push and shove.
'Ooh, all together, ooh, all together.'
Salford had its main faces. My mate Little Dessie was one of the young kids at this time, the same age as me but from the other side of town.

> Little Dessie: *Tommy Fellows, known as the Dog, was one of the main lads. He was there all the way through and he loved it. Then there was a kid called Roger Dunn, a right handsome bastard but hard as nails, and Ronnie Youd – you just didn't get up when he hit you. In fact there were loads. They would go together on a coach from their area and we were like the next lot of kids. In those days it was not an organised fighting mob. We didn't just go for a fight, this was Manchester United. It was your life.*

Harry the Dog – not to be confused with the Millwall character of the same name – was another face, from Stretford. Harry was a nasty brute and he loved it. Like Jeff Lewis, George Lyons, Dave Willis and others, he had a reputation as a fearsome fighter and everyone knew him.

Gradually the shared experience of Old Trafford began to unify the rival mobs. As the gangs began to attend not just home games but also to travel away together, they became even tighter. Suddenly everyone was together on the football specials, the chartered trains used on match days to ferry fans around the rail system. You could argue that the football special actually started football violence, because it put all the thugs together.

London was the best: Euston Station, special due in at 12.30. That was the drill. You'd have thousands of United fans from London and elsewhere waiting for it to pull in. The arrival of the special would be the signal for a couple of hours of mayhem. They would smash the place up every time.

One example was a game against Crystal Palace, which we lost 5–0. I went down with my cousin John. Everyone seemed to be pissed up and when we went on the tube train, they smashed it to bits. Adults were swinging on the straps and kicking the roof in. I was baffled. I was up for mischief but this was grown men going mental. We got so far and the train couldn't go any further; it was literally wrecked.

In the spring of 1972 the Red Army invaded north London on a trip to Arsenal. One newspaper reported:

> A thousand of their supporters marched from Kings Cross Station up the main road skirting the Monmouth estate to the stadium. On the way they broke windows, smashed cars, threw rocks and swore at passers-by. Scattered groups of local youths shouted resistance – from a safe distance. At the end of the day the Streftford End had not only 'taken' the North Bank, but the whole of this part of north London.

The Stretford End was one thing that brought us together, the football specials another. A third was our hatred for Man City. Many of us had City-supporting mates or relatives, but on derby days friendship went out the window. City went through a golden period on the pitch at the turn of the decade, which made the rivalry all the more intense.

My first Manchester derby was in November 1971. The score was 3–3 and there were absolute murders in the ground. United's louts had a belief that they always had to go on the Kippax. For this game everyone turned up outside there and City were waiting inside. We started to pile over the turnstiles and they were on us but we all kept steaming in. Hundreds were there and you had to fight your way up. Eventually the sheer weight of United fans saw us pushing up and occupying a large section. Outside   it was kicking off everywhere around there – Whitworth Park, Claremont Road, all the back streets and ginnels. That set the tone for many years to come.

City had some very hard lads in the Seventies and were one of the top mobs. There would be confrontations in the town or in and around the ground as well as inside, and you always had to be on your toes. But they never came to Old Trafford as a fighting force. They never came out at the end of the game, screaming up Warwick Road, looking for it. That was the challenge. We would always have to go and find them.

We would fill up the city centre before we played them. On one occasion I joined what must have been 2,000 Reds setting off from town on the march down Oxford Road to their ground. As we neared Manchester Royal Infirmary I looked up at a bus and saw my PE teacher from school. I was with my classmate Gary Jones and when he caught our eye we gave him a raised-fist salute. What the fuck.

* * *

FUNNILY ENOUGH, BY the early Seventies some journalists were writing that football hooliganism had passed its peak. As the skinheads grew out their hair and adopted a smoother look, and as some of the original mid-Sixties terrace leaders got older and settled down with the wife, kids and mortgage, there were those who believed the worst days were fading. One of them was a *Sunday Times* reporter I later got to know, Chris Lightbown.

He wrote a piece claiming 'football hooliganism is all but over' but he warned that 'the big uncertainty is the younger generation who, so far, hardly stand boot-high to their predecessors . . . if the new generation becomes involved in football violence, then it will be because they find themselves expected to carry on the tradition of their elders.'

That piece could have been written about me, except I wasn't doing what I did because it was expected of me but because I wanted to. I had tasted that excitement and I wanted more. I and others of that new generation would serve our apprenticeship between 1972 and 1974. Sometimes we would be attacked, sometimes chased, sometimes done in. Usually we would be doing the chasing. But all the time we were learning.

In the 1972–3 season I went to every game at Old Trafford. It was the season United struck their first major blow against the Scousers, charging across the pitch from the Stretford End to get them.

George Lyons: *I have never used a weapon, but the Scousers always used them, even back in the Sixties. When you got chased down Scotty Road they'd take your money, coats, even your shoes.*

Jeff Lewis was one of the main lads. We looked up to Jeff. We'd had a bit of a hiding at Liverpool and United weren't playing very well, we had Wynn Davies and Ted MacDougall playing for us. Scousers always went in the Scoreboard End so the lads thought, right, we'll go in there this time. We got together, about sixty of us, outside the Scoreboard. Jeff Lewis said, 'Wait till five to three.' And then we steamed into them. It was the side to the left, by the Scoreboard Paddock. We steamed in and they were knackered – they couldn't go anywhere because of the fences. Some of them went on the pitch and jumped into the paddock but then the lads from the paddock got them. Then the Stretford End came across, several hundred of them, and the Scousers had to scatter. They stopped the match for ten minutes. We gave them a right pasting that day. It was good.

A night not at Elland Road was an altogether different experience; Leeds and Everton were about the two most violent places you could go in those days. Getting to the ground was not a problem, as I went on the special escorted by a cousin who was ten years older than me. It was after the game that we took our lives in our hands. What was different there was you had the remnants of the Yorkshire Clockwork Orange fan club, dressed in their bibs and braces, a different world even then, but that's Leeds. At the end of the game they came to the back of our 'cowshed' stand and got chased out but to me they looked intimidating in their strange clobber, and a lot of our usual lads weren't there because they were 'working'. Even now some people will find excuses to avoid Leeds.

We came out into a pitched battle, and silly cunts like me with red and white scarves stood out like Belisha beacons. Coppers on horseback were yelling instructions, trying to control the various elements of the crowd.

'Go right, United.'

'Escort this way, coaches that way.'

We started walking up the road. I knew Leeds fans were mingling in with us and we all had heads on springs but nothing happened. Then we got level with a big park on our left, with railings running the length of it. We'd passed it on the way in and the flowerbeds were in full summer bloom, a riot of colour. Now it was dark and eerie. Hundreds of figures began to emerge from the gloom of this park. They were shadows at first, then became real and horrible as they loomed towards us. In no time they were on top of us.

In a click of the fingers, there were no United fans. They'd gone. All that was left were me and my cousin, who tried to protect me from this swirling horde of Clockwork Orange maniacs, with their boots and bowler hats and painted faces. He went down straight away and they put the boot into him.

'Leeds! Leeds! Leeds!'

No-one would help us; you couldn't help yourself. I had no choice but to run into the road and grab the saddle of a police horse as it ran around trying to stop the melee. I wasn't letting go. I lost sight of my cousin and eventually of any other United fans. There was no shout, no, 'Come on, hold it', because this wasn't the soccer thug special. The horse was whipping me around   but I was not leaving it. In the panic I didn't realise I still had my scarf on and it was drawing them to me like moths to a flame. Even the copper was shouting, 'Fuck off, get away,' as he tried to gallop off.

Eventually we made the end of the park. There was chaos everywhere, people running when they didn't even know why. The horse finally ran off and I took off my scarf but instead of slinging it – it would have been dishonour if I'd lost it – I tucked it inside my coat under one of my arms.

It was still a couple of miles to the station and my knees were buckling. Then I heard the dreaded, 'Where are you from?'

'I'm from Leeds,' I replied, trying to front it.

This kid tugged at my coat but opened the wrong side and could see nothing. He was expecting to see a scarf hidden in there.

'Yeah, he's Leeds,' he told his mates. I couldn't be a United fan, because the Red Army wore their colours till they died, didn't they? When I got further down the road, I slung the scarf.

I reached the station without having spoken to a single Man United fan on the way. Most of them were already on the train. They had been scattered and chased everywhere. My cousin was in one of the compartments with a sore face and the knees torn out of his trousers. But I was dead happy because we had won 1-0 and I had escaped a butchering.

The station was oddly quiet. Then the coppers came up.

'Get your shutters down and get on the floor. We're leaving now.'

We had just left the station when:

Boom!

Smash!

Crack!

Two hundred yards from the station Leeds were all there again, throwing everything at us. The windows went and the shutters were coming through. A mile further on, when the bombardment had finished, the coppers came round and said, 'Okay, put the shutters up.'

It would be quite a few years before we got our act together at Leeds, but eventually we would.

CHAPTER THREE

THE WAR WAGON

AUGUST 1973 AND our first game of the season was away to
Arsenal, who had won the Double two seasons before. A
spectacular turnout was guaranteed.

Some jibbed the midnight down to Euston, robbed the cafes,
robbed the milkmen and waited for the Army to arrive. A few
Arsenal mooched around Euston. Yowdy from Salford panned
one and they ran off. Then things started to liven up. That day
you not only had Arsenal coming down to Euston to have a go,
but also Tottenham were leaving from Euston to go to Coventry,
while Chelsea were down the road at Kings Cross waiting to
travel to Derby County. For the first day of the season, it was a
hooligans' paradise.

Tottenham were seen off; they could not get into Euston. The
lads chased a load of them down in the direction of Euston
Square. Some jumped on a bus to try to escape and were being
pulled off and banjoed. The bus driver lost the plot, got off his
double-decker waving a blade about and stabbed a United fan,
an incident that became headline news. Bedlam. Lads trying to
get the knife off him, some wanting to kill him, the bus being
rocked, sirens going, cops fighting people in the road, traffic
brought to a halt. Next came the march to Kings Cross to attack
the Chelsea special. Hundreds of United got to the station,

blasted through the police and drove the Chelsea all over their platform. It was absolutely glorious.

Finally it was time to get to the ground. All the heads were there for this one – Pancho, the Prices from Ashton, Big Dave from Warrington, Jeff Lewis – while a mob of the young wannabes jibbed into the away end. The main United mob always went in the North Bank, and sure enough the usual scrummage and flying fists could be seen. This was the cue for the younger lads to jump out of the away end and run across the pitch to join in. And this was before the game had even started.

That season, I tried to go to every game and remember missing only one, away to Coventry, because I had broken my foot at school on the Friday. They put it in plaster but didn't give me any crutches. I tried to insist on going with a brush under my arm but my mam went mad and I was grounded.

A week later, on December 22, I had my crutches and went to Liverpool with about 170 others on the special. At Lime Street they put us on buses to the ground and as we drove along Scotty Road the Scousers were lining the pavements making threatening gestures. I was on the top deck at the back and a few other young ones like Derek Whittaker and Coco put the back window through and started slinging the seats out at them.

We got escorted to Anfield but then let off the buses, which unfortunately parked on the other side of the Kop. This always baffled me. Inside the ground was horrendous. My mate Vinny McLaughlin and I were in the Anfield Road End, where there was no segregation. My brother had a blade pulled on him at half-time and had to leave. The Scousers were coming in at United at the top but United were holding their own. Downstairs at the bars and toilets they were fighting like animals. You could hear the distant thunder inside.

After the game I had to get off – there was no mob walking

out together at this one, it was every man for himself. The Scousers often hung around the ground in gangs so even if you came out early they got you. One kid I knew was caught on his own on a corner and whacked in the face with a chain. I ended up jumping on a bus with Vinny and it was so dodgy we couldn't even speak. We got to Lime Street before most of the United and of course we got sussed by a few scallies inside the station. Even though I was on crutches, they wanted to do me in. I had one crutch and Vinny had the other and had to swing it to keep the vermin away before help arrived.

On New Year's Day, and still on crutches, I was off again, hitching to Queens Park Rangers from the Knutsford roundabout with Vinny. We didn't have a pot to piss in. We were freezing in the fog, must have been potty, and who should pull up but a vicar. He took us so far and bought us something to eat, which often happened in those days. After a couple more lifts we made it there and met all the lads in London.

I don't remember any trouble at the game, but coming back we had just got off the tube at Euston when crates, bottles and luggage trolleys came down the stairs. It was Arsenal. Everyone went up and at them, with me hobbling behind. It was murder. By the time I had got out of the tube station the Arsenal had been cleared away and United were running around Euston, causing havoc.

With every match I was becoming more streetwise and tougher. I was learning how crowds behaved, how fights developed, what sort of behaviour got what sort of results. It was, if you like, a college of football hooliganism and I was going to graduate with a master's degree. Each game was a lesson.

* * *

IN THE DAYS when few young people owned cars, and coaches were not widely used on match days, the travelling football fan had a limited number of transport options: the football special train, the ordinary service train, the hired van, or the hitchhiker's thumb. For a few years the football special would be the most talked about method, but we had already noticed that it limited your range of movement and the police always knew when and where you were arriving. Sometimes we wanted a different way of getting in and out of a town.

A youth worker called Andy Davies bought the old cop shop near my house, and wanted to convert it. As we all hung about in a crowd around the shops next door, it was in his interests to talk to us so we wouldn't trash the gaff. Andy's job was to monitor young people who would not join youth clubs. He knew how to approach us and not talk down to us. He soon discovered what we were all into and it fascinated him. In truth, Andy was a classic trendy-liberal wally, a clueless do-gooder who we took for a ride. He couldn't understand this football thing and why everyone wanted to kick hell out of each other, but he seemed to get a real kick out of studying our antics.

After a while, he bought a bright yellow wagon that had been used as a portable canteen by British Rail. It was like a big army truck. He ripped out everything inside and had benches fixed to the floor in the back to sit on. You could get up to sixteen sitting down and another ten or fifteen would pile into the open space, sometimes with mattresses thrown on the floor. Another eight could pile in the big cab at the front. The infamous Wythenshawe War Wagon was born.

The War Wagon made us stand out as a mob because no-one else travelled that way at that time. Soon more and more kids off the estate wanted to come with us. Older lads joined in too and on some trips we filled a box van with bodies as well as the War Wagon. Eventually that would lead me to hire coaches to cope with the demand.

Andy used the trips to further himself with his bosses. He told them a lot of crap about how he was helping the youth of the area and even got me in the local paper saying it would be terrible to stop him running the trips after he got in a bit of trouble for association with us and taking us to matches. I had to back him up, saying there was no violence, this man looked after us, we were just a group of fun-loving kids and he had reformed us – though he was actually making us worse.

What he unwittingly did was help to fuel our activities and get us from A to B. When the police got involved he used to smooth it over by saying we were being looked after by him, that we were under the auspices of the Education Department and were under-privileged kids. The police would go easy and simply ask that he keep a tighter hold on us. The times we used to laugh and take the piss out of him because the cops would often ring up his bosses and give him a bollocking on the Monday and I would always reassure him we would behave next time, but he was sucked in. It was destined to end in tears.

The first time I went to Aston Villa was on the War Wagon, with fifteen or so lads of a similar age, fourteen to seventeen. First we planned a visit to the off-licence in our local Co-op store in Wythenshawe. It opened at nine o'clock. We got the youth worker to park round the corner, and when the store opened we all rushed in and literally climbed over shelves, grabbing litres of cider, running off and jumping into our getaway vehicle. Andy Davies put his foot down and scrambled round the estate hoping the police didn't catch us. How on earth a big yellow British Rail van didn't get a pull before we reached the motorway is beyond me.

By the time we reached Birmingham, with not a clue where we were or where we were going, every one of us was smashed out of his head on cider. The brains in charge decided that dropping us in the city centre was a good idea. We fell out and start giving it the big one. Within two minutes I had collapsed over a stall which must have jumped in my path. A friendly passing policeman kindly handcuffed me as I lay on the floor too pissed to move.

Not another thing do I remember until the sergeant woke me in my cell at 7pm, telling me my 'social worker' was here to take me home. No charges, nothing; the only thing that happened was that the youth worker – who had promoted himself to social work – was told to keep a better eye on me and the others. I soon found out how lucky I had been as the rest of them told me they had been chased for miles, staggering around housing estates and having to get on their toes constantly. We all thought in those days you could put on a United scarf and do what you wanted, but not so.

Another moody place we visited in the War Wagon was Middlesbrough. We were all drunk by the time we got there and bumped into Tommy Docherty and his staff in a hotel before the game. He was a good guy, the Doc. Andy Davies left the bus near a park and they jammed us in a corner of the ground. Most of the lads I'd travelled with could by this time barely stand. It was pretty hairy out on the streets but I made it back to the War Wagon with the youth worker, only to see ten of the lads, offering out a similar number of Boro. Next thing, they were all fighting in the street. I piled straight in and we soon fucked them off. Fortunately no other gangs of Boro were around; we were drunk, reckless and didn't realise the danger we were in.

You had to be on your mettle when you went to the North-east, whereas we always treated the Midlands as a beano. Not that you wouldn't get trouble there (see Chapter Nine) but we would swamp the place and the atmosphere was different. West Brom was one of our favourite places, and for one of my first visits there I went with the main mob on the train while the older Wythenshawe lads went in the War Wagon. They were all beer monsters and basically were going for the drink.

The train mob had the usual idea – 'Let's go in their end' – but it was dodgy trying to get in through the police. Eventually a few of us sneaked in and got onto the terracing. It was about 2pm. A lot more congregated up at the top right hand side as we faced the pitch, about 150–200, no scarves, all dead quiet. No-one had sussed us. By this time we had perfected the art of taking an end.

'What are we going to do?' asked one of the lads.

'Here's what we're going to do,' I said, then roared, 'United!' 'United!'

The chant caused a space to open and there we stood. We had the advantage of being at the top of the terrace and couldn't be moved. Then we went for it, arms and legs windmilling into those nearest to us. The police were quickly there, breaking up the fighting and eventually forcing us down the terrace and out onto the pitch. After a few seconds of exchanging abuse and gestures with the furious West Brom crowd, we were marched around the pitch and put in United's end.

At the side of the home terrace was a gangway and ten minutes later up came the older lads from the War Wagon, bladdered. They knew they had missed the boat by staying in the pub but had decided to go into West Brom's end anyway and now came flying down, being attacked but fighting them off. There were a few big beer bellies among these lads and they were having a right go, while we were all laughing and cheering them on from the other end of the ground. They finally got to the bottom to the fence and tried to climb over but kept getting pulled back. Eventually the police booted them out, by which time they had taken a proper smacking. They enjoyed the usual heroes' reception from the United end.

'Reds are here, Reds are there, Reds are fucking every-where . . .'

'United aggro, United aggro, hello, hello . . .'

Coming out, we charged down the road to get back in their end and it was crap, like they didn't want it. They weren't good enough.

*   *   *

BACK IN WYTHENSHAWE, football was all there seemed to be. It gave our lives meaning. Our gang was impatient for the thrill of match day and in the pre-season we found our own entertainment, based on the match-day experience. We decided we would take the train from Gatley to Alderley Edge, where all the posh bastards lived, and cause trouble. It was, if you like, our imitation of the Red Army's marauding trips away. So every Saturday morning we would arrive in Gatley for 9am and get the train. This became our 'football special'. As soon as we arrived we would run out of the station, kick over displays outside the shops, run through the town centre and then disperse into the hills.

The first time we did it, there was about twenty of us. Steve Hesford, who loved acting up, grabbed a huge melon off a table outside a fruit and veg shop and decide it was a ball. He threw it up in the air and launched a boot into it. The melon exploded, bits flying everywhere – mainly over us. The bloke from the shop came running after him but Hesford was roaring with laughter. We decided his stalls were going over in the street, just like on a match day, then off we went, down the street, singing and shouting threats to the toffs.

We did this for a few weeks and would occasionally bump into a few lads who we would slap about and chase around. What I didn't notice was that this group got larger and larger each week as the word was obviously spread about these louts from Wythenshawe. We were too busy getting some action and doing some looting to notice.

Our group grew too. Walking down Crossacres Road to Gatley at 8.30 on Saturday mornings, we were being joined by lads coming from Peel Hall and Woodhouse Park. As we neared Gatley, the Benchill Mob would be coming down Hollyhedge Road right on time. The mob grew so big that we were filling a

39

full carriage. We were now running into some good opposition in Alderley Edge, and because we were mainly in our early teens and our rivals were usually older, we were tooling up – and made sure we had the right stuff.

Again we copied what we knew the football hooligans of the time carried. *Nunchakus*, two kung fu sticks joined by a chain, were plentiful as you could make them at school. We also had metal throwing stars, again made in the school metalwork shop – the *Daily Mirror* ran an exposé saying the stars were being cut in a workshop at Yew Tree High School in Wythenshawe, after one of them had slashed a hole in a bobby's helmet at Notts County. The *nunchakus* were all the rage, as the TV series *Kung Fu* was on telly and Bruce Lee films were massive at the box office. It was unbelievable that everyone who had hold of these swore blind that they had been taught by Bruce Lee himself, but true to form you would roll about laughing after any trouble had finished as you recalled how you'd seen your pal standing in the street swinging these things about, only for him to smash them on his own head.

The thing was, on a match day up and down the country there were hundreds of people doing the same thing, standing there in flares, tight jeans and boots on, some in star jumpers, some with flares on their shirt collars, Crombie coats, budgie jackets, swinging these things and not one could use them properly. Despite what they believed, not one looked like Bruce Lee; in fact they looked proper idiots and were nearly always the ones to get twatted first by the opposition, as your mates wouldn't stand near you in case you hit them with the sticks. Well you live and learn.

There had to be an end to our activities in Alderley Edge and it came in true football fashion. The train was halted one Saturday morning in Wilmslow for twenty minutes and we hadn't a clue why. We piled off, full of intent to smash anything or anyone who got in our way – and found what looked like the whole Cheshire police force waiting for us. They came from the waiting rooms, running down the stairs from the railway bridge and jumping out from concrete pillars to halt us in our tracks. As thousands of hooligans up and down the country have experienced, we were pushed up against the walls, searched and generally given a rough time.

The police were out in force and we were going nowhere but back. Forty to fifty coppers escorted us across, not so much to prevent us from getting away as to stop what seemed like a right tasty firm of locals from kicking our heads in. We later found out that the local youths had had enough, and gangs from Nantwich, Northwich and surrounding areas had descended on Alderley Edge for revenge. I for one was grateful that the police were there, as it was us that needed them. I would later experience a similar feeling on match days, when things go wrong and you have underestimated the enemy. You start joking then with the police that if it wasn't for them you would have leathered the opposition, but we've all put on that bravado shit.

One outcome of this was we decided that Manchester city centre, and in particular Piccadilly, was now the place to be on Saturday mornings. That was where the United fans gathered before every home game, and no-one could ever take the city centre – or so we thought.

* * *

MARCH 9, 1974, was an FA Cup weekend. Unfortunately we had already been knocked out, and as Glasgow Rangers were also out of the Scottish Cup, some genius decided to invite them down for a Saturday afternoon 'friendly'. In my naivety, I didn't realise that to the hooligans of both teams, this was much more than a game of football. This was England v. Scotland for the title decider.

On this day we missed the gathering in town in the morning,

as we made one of our hooligan excursions to Alderley Edge. We then came in on the train to Oxford Road, where we changed for Old Trafford station. The sight that greeted me and the dozen lads with me was completely novel. All around us were hundreds of men, cheering and singing, pissed out of their heads – and they were Rangers fans. This was something I had never expected to see in my hometown. Away supporters in Manchester, on their way to Old Trafford? They'll get smashed all over, surely?

The problem was, it was my pals and I who were likely to get smashed in first. We were crammed in a carriage with them, wearing our scarves but wishing we weren't, looking and feeling pretty sorry for ourselves. The saving grace was our youth: these pissed-up jocks, to their credit, just took the piss and joked with us.

The scene I witnessed on arriving at Old Trafford can only be described as mental. There it was, right in front of me on the forecourt up Warwick Road: nothing but Jocks, and they were causing mayhem. The Jocks had poured into town as though it was a cup final. I didn't know then about the bigotry towards us. Only later was I told that they considered us a Catholics' club and associated us with Celtic, so we were like a red rag to a bull: we hate the English, we hate Celtic, we hate Man United, bingo, riot time – and a riot is what it was. It simply was not safe, and for the one and only time outside our ground, I quickly got off. The more violent of our fans often went in the Scoreboard End, and eventually the notorious K Stand above, to attack the away supporters, but today that was not an option. The only safe place for us at our age was the Stretford End.

Packed into the Stretford, we looked across the pitch at this mass of swaying blue. It was awesome, a scene you dream of being in. I hadn't seen an away following that big. The noise, energy and raw emotion coming from them set your hair on end. You knew it was going to blow and needed only one thing.

On he came, a stumbling, swaying Scottish drunk, over the wall and across the pitch. The crowd urged him on but his brain wasn't in gear with his legs and it took him ages to reach the halfway line. It was all a laugh, with both ends shouting approval and willing him on to his goal. Whatever that goal was, someone had decided he wasn't going to reach it. A United fan was running towards him. Immediately you could see others coming on the pitch from the Rangers end; they knew what the United fan's intentions were and were trying to reach Braveheart before he did. This sparked a similar reaction from the Stretford End, with some of the hardier lads doing the same to save their hero.

The United fan reached Braveheart and prolapsed him with one flying Doc Marten boot to his chest.

In no time there must have been 100–150 scrapping it out in the middle of the pitch. When I look back it was comical, because you had people who were dressed as though they were from idiot world, white butchers' coats running backwards and forwards, long-haired thugs with their Docs on. There were no police at the Stretford End, as they were trying to hold back the mad Jocks, so the Reds had the upper hand and were giving out a few good slaps. Yours truly decided he was now hard enough, time to join in, so I led my little gang onto the pitch. We had reached no further than the edge of the penalty area when we stopped in our tracks and had to retreat in a lively manner before the rest of the United fans trampled us. The reason for our abrupt about-turn was simple: the Jocks had broken through and were heading our way.

Everyone was now back in the Stretford End and I wasn't sure we could hold these Jocks. It's hard to explain why the Jocks didn't try to jump into our end, but those brave enough probably couldn't get in, as everyone was desperately slinging punches at them. All this was happening three-quarters of an hour before the game and it seemed that it would never end, but eventually the police cleared the pitch; what I mean is, they left loads of people writhing on the ground in agony. The police had taken a beating early on but were now up to the task and they got their own back. They had solid wooden truncheons and they were smashing skulls in. When they had their victims on the floor they were giving it them proper. That's always been one thing about our police: they give you a good kicking. They would probably be better at it than most of the hoolies.

The ground was only half full – the crowd was 25,000 – with the two ends packed but both sides virtually empty. That didn't last as the Jocks now tried to come across the seats. Little gangs made their way towards the Stretford End and you could see pockets of United fans willing to have it with them. These groups engaged and started fighting, with not one from either side backing down. It made great viewing, as it went on for ages and no-one was going to let their side down. We again roared our approval, urging our boys on, until the police chased each group back towards their own supporters. You'd see some lads disappearing on their way back as they fell between the seats and this only made the others run faster, as the plod made sure you got a kicking.

The Jocks were going crazy, but the fighting was certainly not one-sided. When the Rangers manager was asked to go on the pitch to calm down his fans, he replied, 'Why should I go out there when the only people I can see being brought in by the St John Ambulance are in the blue, red and white of Rangers?'

The game went by in a blur and the talk was of going to the city centre, as there would be loads more trouble. I heard tales of gangs of United trying to take on the Jocks before the game and it seemed to me things had not gone our way. For once in my life, I thought better of it, and my little gang decided to make our way home. We passed the Scoreboard End, where the Jocks were still locked in. You could hear them pounding and screaming to get out and it was only a matter of time before they kicked down the gates. I could actually see the gates buckling

and knew that if I was there when they flew open.
So that day my Doc Martens were used only to sp
back to Wythenshawe, to plan our next match.

* * *

WE PLAYED EVERTON on a Tuesday evening in late April,
facing relegation. As a child I was very independent – from the
age of ten I had wandered all over Manchester on my own – but
every now and then, for no apparent reason, my mam would
kick off on me and stop me going out. This baffled me, because
she knew I wasn't involved in any skulduggery on the estate. On
this particular afternoon I came home from school to find it was
one of those days when my old dear decided I wasn't going out.
Maybe I hadn't done one of my chores. When I protested that I
had to go to the match, she forced me into her bedroom and
locked the door. But nothing was going to stop me. The bay
window was below her bedroom window and I climbed out
onto the top of it, then jumped into the garden and made my
escape. I caught the bus to Victoria and was soon queuing for
the 5.30 special, with loads of faces I knew, everyone dead
happy.

I was on the first of two specials. We pulled up at Lime Street
and all came charging out. There were some notorious blocks of
flats around the station in those days and the first fight started
there. Scousers appeared from this bombsite of a place but we
chased them all off – which a full football special should, let's
face it. That was the only incident before the game. We paid in
and watched United win the match 1–0.

When we came out it was dark. This was it: pitch black,
Scousers, everyone watching for blades. We were directed to the
road where buses were supposed to be waiting to take us back to
the train station, but there was no escort. We managed to reach
the buses without incident and I was with all the usual faces,

in Wythenshawe, Salford and Collyhurst. People had just
ed piling on the buses when the shout went up.

'Come on, we're marching.'

It was George Lyons. I couldn't understand why we were
pushing our luck – I thought it was daft – but the shout had
gone up, so we ended up with a mob of 150 of us marching in
the direction of the city centre. A lot sensibly stayed on the
buses but of course I had to go with the mob.

We reached the end of Stanley Park and everyone was tense –
there had still been no shout from Everton. We crossed the road
and came to some houses on our left. And that was when they
struck. Out of a side street they charged, hundreds of them,
down the hill in the dark, and blitzed right through us. I was at
the front so there was no going back for me, with the weight of
bodies behind, but there was no standing and fighting either
because it was right on top – there were loads of them. We were
fighting Merseyside, not just Everton – they had all turned out
to get the Mancs.

They steamed through us. Those at the back must have gone
backwards but we could only go forwards and somehow found
ourselves in a bit of space. We faced a long walk back – only
there wasn't any walking, because they were on our backs all the
way. It was one long chase: from the moment they ran into us we
never stopped running because they never gave us a minute to
rest. Even when the mob behind us slowed, others were coming
out of all the little estates on Scotty Road and were on every
corner, throwing bricks. The group I was with must have been
fifty- or sixty-handed and by the time we got halfway down
Scotty Road it was thirty-handed. People had ducked away or
fallen over and been caught. Occasionally we stopped to try to
help someone but we couldn't hold the Scousers off for long.
They had the numbers out that night.

There were five casualties slashed. I saw two get cut myself:
one was caught on some grassy banking and one was right in our

crowd. We couldn't do anything about it. One was cut in the shoulder and one down his front – we had turned to have it with thirty of them and this lad came in and striped him. There were no police with us – the Scouse coppers always fucked you off anyway. 'Well, you shouldn't have come,' was their favourite saying. They always used to search us even though we weren't the ones with the tradition of carrying blades – it was unheard of for us in those days. We were fighters, there for the fight, but the Scousers always carried knives. They wouldn't stand and fight without them. They were there to maim. We found it a perverse way of living: they seemed to gloat and glory in disfiguring people.

After the second cutting we legged it further down the road and came across a cop Land Rover parked on Scotty. We ran towards it. People were fighting everywhere and we were trying to keep together. I was a young kid and no-one was catching me. This Land Rover drove up alongside us and partially shielded us from the bombardment of missiles on one side.

Then we came to an expanse of flat, open land and could now be seen clearly from miles away. It was an open invitation and Scousers already knew to line the route. We ran for our lives. Liverpool had had it at Old Trafford the year before when United invaded the pitch and got them in the Scoreboard End. This was payback time for the Scousers.

As we legged across this waste ground, my training shoe came off. I stopped but a group of Scousers were right behind me and the Land Rover was driving away. I had to bend down and half hop, half hobble, trying to put my shoe on, working it over my heel. The Land Rover eventually gave up as we got near the city centre and the few of us still together ran straight through town as though the hounds of hell were on our heels and burst into Lime Street station.

It was chaos. People were turning up thrashed, clothes stolen, bloodied, beaten. Then the train got bricked on the way back. I would often wonder later why I climbed out of my mam's bedroom window, because there was no enjoyment that night at all.

* * *

OUR FORM THAT season had been dire and we went into our last home game staring relegation in the face. We still had a chance, but we needed to beat Manchester City while Norwich had to get a result against Birmingham. The term fever pitch hardly begins to do justice to the atmosphere among the 57,000 fans inside the ground. We were in the Scoreboard, which was supposed to be their end, but there were fewer than 2,000 of them in the two sections nearest to the Scoreboard Paddock, and they were mainly shedheads, not hooligans. They weren't a gang. I was in the ground at 1.15 and we occupied the section behind the net that City should have occupied. We took the main sections in the middle and to the right and booted out the first City fans to come in. As more United came in, we knew who was where.

After that initial jockeying for territory, the fighting on the terraces died down. We went underneath, to the back of the stand, and a fight started there. I had a face-to-face with a City fan, one guy, our scarves flying about until it was broken up. The fighting actually started underneath at about 1.15 because I was on the terracing by 1.30. I think we had four sections and they had two, with United fans in amongst them.

Half-time came and we tried to get them again underneath and there was some trouble but it was quickly sorted out. Then, with seven minutes to go, Denis Law scored for them. Everyone was jumping up and hopping over the barriers and diving into City's section. The City fans seemed to disappear – they had this great ability to do that – as the Stretford End emptied onto the pitch. By then we were already on our way to Division Two, as the Birmingham result had gone against us, but I suppose some people thought that if they got the game abandoned it might somehow mean something.

I came out and didn't see a single City fan. I can't blame them really, as everyone was going crazy.

* * *

OUR FINAL GAME of the season was away to Stoke City and we had more fighting there. Stoke gave us some really good goes in the mid Seventies. They had a habit of coming at you through that graveyard, and especially at night games it was unnerving; they appeared from nowhere. In the early Seventies we'd think nothing of going in their end but as the years went by it became a much stiffer challenge. They would also come flying at you in that tunnel by the train station; I've been charged by 3–400 of them down there. They were a solid group who tended to congregate at a couple of specific boozers and they were game. They all knew each other and their accent was distinctive. But they were another firm I don't ever remember coming to Old Trafford.

The season 1973–4 had been my apprenticeship. Despite terrifying visits to Elland Road and Goodison Park, I thought it was great. It was part of life, more and more experiences. I was going with all the lads and it made me more aware. I was ready. I wasn't a baby any more; I was in there. Now it was expected of me and that was what I wanted.

That summer was also a turning point in my life, as I officially left school at sixteen. In reality I had left the previous September; I just got up and walked out. Even though I was in the top class all the way through, school wasn't for me. There were better things to do. I blagged my way onto a bricklaying course at Manchester Building College by saying I was eighteen, even though I was fifteen, but by Christmas the Education

Department had rumbled me because I hadn't been able to produce a P45. They could have done me for truancy, but instead they said, 'You're better off where you are, at least you're learning a trade.' I was also earning £12 a week, out of which I had to give my mam a tenner – and she was getting family allowance and blagging me that she wasn't! However, the college were not happy that I'd had them over in my interview, so instead of giving me a certificate and apprenticeship at the end of the course, they fucked me off.

After working part-time on an adventure playground in Wythenshawe, I ended up as a youth worker for Manchester Youth Service. They wanted to place people in youth clubs but that wasn't my idea of youth work. Instead I took up my own project – which was unheard of – working with the homeless and the runaways in town. I would go out at 10pm and stay in town all night, hanging around the cafes and mixing with them. I might be chatting in Piccadilly Gardens at 3am. I would often be out until 6am, until the first bus back to Wythenshawe, even though I was only sixteen myself. I would talk to anyone and eventually I would coax many of them into coming back to Wythenshawe to the security of Andy Davies's place, which was a home for them. Then we would try to get in touch with their parents and reassure them that their kids were okay. Sometimes we had a couple of girls and they were very vulnerable. I could talk to them and in the end people got used to me.

So you could say I was streetwise, from a very early age. My experiences at the match – I had endured some terrifying times that season, against the likes of Leeds, Liverpool, Everton and Glasgow Rangers – had also toughened me up. Which was just as well, because United's campaign of terror against the rest of the football world was only just beginning.

In May 1974 the *Daily Mirror*, under the headline 'Soccer's Season of Shame', published the number of arrests of supporters of all twenty-two First Division clubs. Not surprisingly, what it called 'the Stretford Enders' had 100 more arrests than any other set of fans. We were described as 'the worst behaved fans' and 'the team whose visit is most dreaded'. These hooligan league tables were always bollocks to me, but at least this one did reflect how we had misbehaved that season. And worse, far worse, was to come.

CHAPTER FOUR

TOMMY DOC'S
RED ARMY

MANCHESTER UNITED'S YEAR in the Second Division has passed into hooligan legend. What went on in the season 1974-5 will never be repeated. Times have changed, grounds have changed, fans have changed, policing has changed. By the end of the season, people were saying that the Government ran the country for six days a week but Saturdays belonged to the Red Army. Whether you view them as the good old days or the bad old days, we'll never see their like again.

We were the biggest club in the country – possibly the world. Six years earlier we had been champions of Europe. Our finest players – Best, Law, Charlton – were all-time greats in anyone's book. And here we were in Division Two, visiting small grounds with clueless coppers and no segregation. The Red Army was too big to handle, and wherever it went, mayhem ruled.

It began pre-season, with a trip to Hull. We were off the train in time for the first pint to be pulled. I had no thought of trouble that day and treated it as a jolly with the lads, but often when you don't go looking for aggro you find more than normal, and this was one of those days. In the pub were some good lads and we had been in there about one hour and were all relaxed and having the crack when it seemed as though time stopped. One minute banter filled the air, the next the door burst open and a big nutcase stood there with a gang of mates, shouting and waving his arms about.

Deathly quiet was now the order of the day. I couldn't tell what the nutter was saying but Pubby, who is normally a placid chap, took exception to being interrupted in mid flow with some bullshit tale of bedding some bird. He took aim with a beer tray and slung it, directly hitting the nutter. This made everyone wake up to the fact that Hull were there with a firm. Without any more prompting, tables and glasses were hurled in their direction, with everyone now heading for the door. The nutter and his mates were twatted and chased through the door, followed by us. We piled out with half the contents of the pub in our hands and launched them at any lad in the vicinity. As quickly as it started it was over, with Hull disappearing. Strangely it was the only trouble I witnessed that day, maybe because the Red Army was everywhere and Hull didn't show again, as things could only get worse for them. Who knows?

Our first game of the season proper was Leyton Orient away. I hitched. Mindful of the nights I'd been caught out in the cold, I wore my brother's sheepskin coat. I was in London for 4am and waited at Euston because that was always the meeting place. I knew there could be a bit of trouble because one or two London teams were leaving to play away: Arsenal, for example, had to leave St Pancras on their way to Leicester.

A couple of thousand United fans were waiting around Euston by daybreak. These people were my meal ticket as well as my protection; I could always cadge ten bob off one of the older lads. It being mid-August, as the sun rose the temperature began to climb – and there was me stuck with this sheepskin coat, which I couldn't sling because it was my brother's.

At mid-morning, someone said, 'Right, come on, we're going for Arsenal.' They had a fleet of special trains going to Leicester but we already had enough for the assault. Everyone was up and moving slowly off Euston. Some didn't even know where they were going but they followed all the same. The Cockney Reds were organising it because it was their patch and they knew what was going on. They and Arsenal seemed to have a particular rivalry. We decided we had to go for them because they weren't coming for us.

We filled Euston Road as we walked along, marching through the traffic and on both sides of the road. Soon we could see the façade of St Pancras and the ramp with a couple of hundred Arsenal at the top. It all seemed in slow motion. I was with Black Sam, who was a bit older than me, a Cockney and big for his age: a handy lad, game as fuck. We could see Arsenal egging each other on and more and more began to pour out of the station and move down in a wave to meet us. The police were about and were running around St Pancras, trying to prevent a clash. The traffic was in chaos, with cars pointing in all directions. Both sides were soon charging towards each other in broken formation because of the traffic.

I was on a corner with Black Sam and two dozen others when the first contact came. We went in swinging. The Arsenal were big lads and they were roaring, 'Caaam on!' Some seemed to know Sam and made a beeline for him. We had run on ahead of our main mob to get the first and were cut off slightly but we stood our ground and so did they. It was toe to toe, with bodies going over the bonnets of cars and one or two people rolling on the floor. Yet somehow it didn't seem vicious; both sides knew you couldn't afford to be gripped and dragged down.

I have never put the boot in when someone was on the floor – I would try to stop it if they have had enough. If I put someone over with a punch I would carry on to the next one. Don't get me wrong, I have put the boot in when it was needed, but I wasn't brought up that way. If you won a fight, you won it. I never liked bullying. I was cock of my junior school and only had one fight. Once a kid was cowering or not fighting back you had won.

Black Sam was under pressure but I was staying right next to him. He was the trophy for them but we were not backing off. After twenty or thirty seconds of furious scuffling, the police got between us and sent Arsenal back to St Pancras. No-one had won, no-one had lost. If the roads had not been as chaotic it would have been one of the major battles. As it was, I was impressed by both sides.

Then it was a rampage down the road towards Kings Cross. An estimated 10,000 Reds were at the game, breaking down the gates to get in and invading the pitch twice before kick-off. At one stage Matt Busby even appealed over the loudspeaker for calm but instead the Reds broke lumps of concrete from the terraces, bombarded the Orient keeper and tried to rock over the television gantry with commentator Brian Moore inside. We tried to look for a bit of trouble in the ground but found nothing. I became bored. There was no-one to fight properly, it was red hot and I was sweating like mad in my sheepie. I fell asleep in a corner during the game.

*   *   *

FOLLOWING THE PITCH invasions against Man City on the last day of the season, the club erected a steel fence along the perimeter of the Stretford End. This had the unintended effect of banding the lads even more closely together, and a real them against us mentality grew. As the *Observer* newspaper reported:

> The Stretford End . . . is a kind of academy of violence, where promising young fans can study the arts of intimidation. This season the club installed a metal barrier between the fans and the ground. It resembles the sort of cage, formidable and expensive, that is put

up by a zoo to contain animals it needs but slightly fears. Its effect has been to make the Stretford terraces even more exclusive and to turn the occupants into an elite.

The name of the game for the opposition at Old Trafford was to get to the ground in one piece, put on a good show and so claim a 'result'. It was down to the home side to spoil their day and United with their hordes usually did this. We played the dreaded Millwall at home straight after Orient away and there was no firm of them, only the odd couple of lads here and there who kept their heads down, as they knew this was life and death. Everyone was out early that day and Manchester was heaving. You saw lads waiting on every corner with one thing in mind. The story has it that Millwall did have a mob on the train but they were accompanied up by the Cockney Reds, who immediately attacked them when they got off at Piccadilly. When a waiting crowd of Mancs joined in, the Millwall fled to the safety of a nearby fire station, were rounded up by police and were put on the next train home without seeing the game.

I didn't witness that, but whatever the truth, it was an anti-climax. I was disappointed. All the talk had been about these fearless South London maniacs who would take you on regardless of the numbers. We knew we would have to go to their place to make a point. I always kept it in my head that whatever we did at home, the away team would be waiting for us when we were due in their town, and with United having the Red Army travelling all over there were plenty of chances to take revenge.

Incidentally, Harry the Dog became their main face after featuring in a 1977 *Panorama* documentary. He bumped into our own Harry the Dog when a small bunch of United were coming home from Norwich on the train and Millwall got on, returning from some away game. A few words were exchanged and our Harry snarled, 'There's only one Dog on this train.'

The next thing a row broke out and they captured Little Craig and barricaded themselves in the buffet car. Harry fetched the rest of the lads, including Black Sam, Eddie Beef and Co., and started smashing the door to get through to the buffet while Milwall desperately kept it wedged shut. The Millwall, who hadn't realised the quality they were up against, pulled the emergency cord and brought the train to a stop in the middle of nowhere. They were last seen running across open fields.

*   *   *

AUGUST ENDED WITH a trip to Cardiff City. The Taffies were coming off a riot at Bristol and this one got the full media build-up, with Cardiff being described as a 'terror-ridden city' in the *Daily Mirror* and householders being warned to stand guard over their homes. One newspaper called it 'the least long-awaited clash since Boadicea's chariots bumped into the Romans' and researchers have put it down as the first ever game where the pre-match newspaper coverage was more about the threat from the fans than it was about the match. The stage was set.

We hitched the night before from Wythenshawe. Loads hitched that season; you would stand with your scarf dangling from your wrist so people could see, hoping for a friendly Red to pick you up. The plan was always to meet in or around the train station on arrival. It was lovely and warm that morning and I was there for 6am, one of the first to arrive. We went in a café and by 7.30 it was full of United in their colours, with some spilling outside.

Then from somewhere came 'Fuck off!' and we were all at it. A trainload of taffies had come in, probably from the valleys or one of the mining towns, and attacked the café. They were mad blokes. It was all hands to the pump: knives, forks, spoons, plates, mugs – we had to throw everything at them to fuck them off. A cop car pulled up and the fight stopped, but from that moment we knew it was game on.

Everyone stuck around the station and made sure they didn't wander far; we did go for the odd walk but kept each other in sight. Gradually more United arrived and little skirmishes broke out around the edges of the crowd. It was a matter of waiting to get a foothold in the first pub yet by noon the police, who had spent the previous few days erecting special barricades, had virtually cordoned off a section of the city and were trying to keep us together.

Then the big roar went up and United were on the march to the ground. The tartan scarves were out and it was Tommy Doc's red and white army are here and have come to take on the Welsh. No other team could have done it. The Doc Martens were double tight that day. We bounced all the way but there was no mass confrontation; for some reason it didn't happen.

A few of us paid into the Cardiff end. I had never been there before and didn't understand the hatred, but I assumed United would make an effort to go in their end. I went down to the front with Dave Farrell, one of the Prescotts and Dave Walker. They had their scarves hidden under their coats. Straight away we realised we had to get out. It was lunacy. These Welshmen were demented, baying for English blood, and that shocked me. There wasn't a friendly face in the whole end. One word and we would have died. I made the decision to go down to the bottom of the terrace and we got out onto the pitch, even though it was still only 1.30pm. We walked round to the United end.

I can't remember a ball being kicked because I don't think I looked at the pitch. We faced them, they faced us and for ninety minutes it was pure hatred, with everything being slung at each other. Then they started to chant.

'Munich, Munich, Munich.'

The Scouse vermin had started singing about the Munich air

disaster a few years earlier. In those days if you heard a Munich chant it was a riot, no hesitation, and no United fan would condemn you. You hit us where it hurts, we'll hit you. United responded with chants of 'Aberfan', which sent the Welsh mental. It was only sung two or three times but that was all it needed. This Cardiff fan in shorts jumped on the fence, going proper mad, trying to get over at us. He was their figurehead. All the police were at this fence and it nearly went once or twice. You just knew that at the end of the game it was going to be all-out war.

We came out before the end of the game into a park or field at the back of Cardiff's end. There was the kid in the shorts, leading quite a few Cardiff. United went for it. We charged onto the field, the riot started and the kid in the shorts got done in, along with quite a few others. Then the final whistle must have gone because both sides poured out.

I had to be at the front – I was not missing this for anything. This was what it was all about. Both sides tried to get into each other but the police managed to separate them. So now the march back to town was on. The police couldn't keep us apart as we moved away from the ground and into the terraced streets. It was brilliant. At every ginnel we would charge down and as we got to the end and tried to spill out they would swarm from all over and chase us back – then they would charge down at us and we would see them off. People were getting twatted all over the place. It was proper vicious – running down a side street with two half-bricks in your hands and slamming into them. It was almost as though both sides were taking turns to pile in and it continued like that all the way back to the city centre.

It was what dreams are made of.

In the end I got to the train station. Lines of coppers had manoeuvred Cardiff so they couldn't actually come up to the station, but there was still the bus station, another potential flashpoint. A couple of us had a mooch around and found a few of them, bigger and older than us. In the end I had to beat a retreat to the station concourse, thinking I was safe next to the cops. A Cardiff fan walked over and I expected him to give me some gob. Instead the twat butted me, right in front of the coppers. I stayed on my feet but I was in shock. The coppers grabbed me, not him, whacked me over the head and said, 'Go on you English cunt, fuck off.'

My face was still aching when I jumped on the special. It must have been one of the fullest trains ever. No-one was staying in that town; it was enemy territory and no-one wanted to be captured.

Yet Cardiff, I don't know why, didn't come to Old Trafford.

George Lyons: *Cardiff was real violence. I came down from Manchester on the train and one of the lads said it was kicking off all over. We got to the ground and my mate Wils got hit with a brick. He picked it up and went to swing it back and the police nicked him. He got three months. He was one of the first football hooligans to ever be jailed and was on News At Ten. Then they all come at us and we give it them, chased them all over. It was kicking off outside and my mate Dave was getting chased by the police and I tripped one up and he nearly went under a bus. There was windows getting smashed and they had a big crew coming up and we chased them back to the ground, they couldn't chase us because there was too many of us. It was pure violence that day.*

* * *

CARDIFF HAD BEEN unmissable but Millwall away I was not looking forward to. I had a gut-wrenching feeling in my stomach, brought about by lack of enthusiasm from my pals, who all decided that because it was a Monday night game, they couldn't go. A lovely excuse, which always seemed to coincide with the scariest away trips, but this game was being played on my birthday and I couldn't miss it. My last year in school was to see another few days' absence from young O'Neill. It was the one and only time I set out for a match with a bit of a cover story to protect myself; as I began my Sunday night journey to hitchhike to London, I put on my school blazer. I thought that if things went pear-shaped, wearing it could get me out of trouble.

Euston Station at twelve o'clock the next day brought it home to me that this was no normal day for Manchester United. I was on my own. There were none of the usual faces, no hitchhikers, no early drinkers and, above all, no Red Army. This was a blow, as the Red Army was not only my security but also my meal ticket. They kept me in food and drink when I had no money, and I could always tap a bob or two when needed. Not today. My stomach was still churning, made all the worse as it dawned on me that my school blazer would probably be no protection at all.

I had to use my head. All the signs indicated that this might be the time for me – and most of all, United – to get an almighty kicking, something I didn't want to witness. It took all my nerve to keep me at Euston, waiting for the special train from Manchester. As the hours passed, my observations at Euston made me feel worse and worse. On every corner were spies, counting and observing the odd small group of United fans. All day I saw Cockneys roaming around in twos and threes, trying to suss United's tactics. Well, there were no tactics: the few of us that were there could only wait for the special and hope.

It arrived at about 5.45pm and off they came. There was none of the usual running and screaming, only a dignified walk onto the forecourt. I needed the security of the mob so I could relax and enjoy, but it didn't look as though it was going to happen. The lads looked grimly determined; they all knew that a level head was called for. I joined the crowd, determined to stay close to my hero Jeff Lewis and his drinking pals.

We were taken on the tube straight to Millwall. I say taken; what I mean is the 180 on the special and the thirty or forty that had hung around for them went without fuss (something that many of the new age designer-fashion wimps do on a regular basis). Looking good but doing nothing: this was the only time I saw United do that in the Seventies. They had good reason, as the whole of the football thug world was awaiting this confrontation, especially in London.

When we arrived the nerves had proper set in. As the tube doors opened we piled off – to nothing, absolutely nothing. Not that it cheered me up; it only made things worse, as I now expected to be ambushed at any time. I really thought we were goners when we entered what was known as Dangerous Alley, and this was aptly named, as you couldn't see the end of it due to its curved shape. It was an alley with a wall eight foot high on both sides, with glass embedded in concrete. There was no escape but again nothing happened. We came to the ground. No baying mob, no bricks, nothing.

I went inside and got on the terracing. Fuck me, I wanted to go home there and then. I have never seen a rougher, more unwelcoming bunch of blokes. Every face was looking around and eyeballing each other, looking for the giveaway sign. At least the school blazer worked, as all these horrible dockers took no notice of me. I wandered around, hoping to get with some Reds, but the ones I came across ignored me. It was the right thing for them to do, as this ground was at boiling point. It seemed every thug in London was at this shithole, wanting to get their revenge on the Red Army, and it didn't take long for their chance to come.

In the opposite end to us, below the goal, some brave but foolhardy souls put up the chant of 'United!' Everyone went barmy, trying to get round there, pushing and pulling each other, but for most of the Millwall thugs it was a waste of time. By the time they got to the scene the singers sang no more. I was ill as I witnessed from afar those foolish few being smashed to the floor and stomped. They were done for and there was nothing anyone could do. Some were taken away on stretchers. I haven't heard to this day any mention of who was beaten up in there or who was actually in that end but they took a brutal pasting.

Incredibly, at one point during the game a laughing and pissed-up group of lads from North Manchester and Salford started singing in our end and nothing happened to them. Why, I don't know. I can only believe God was with them, as the ground had 27,000 thugs in that night, when their normal crowd was about 4,500.

Half-time approached and decision time for me. I was not happy with my surroundings and I came to the realisation that luck only lasts for so long. Off I went, over the turnstiles and out, with no looking back as I knew this would attract any London scallies hanging about. Dangerous Alley was avoided and I soon saw New Cross tube station. I was not the only Red there but you could see on their faces that it wasn't over yet. The few minutes we had to wait for the train seemed like eternity but luck stayed with us and we were soon Euston-bound.

A few drinks in the pub back at the station – with my school blazer now carefully hidden from the landlord – brought relief from the tension and through the rest of the evening more fans slowly arrived back. It was still a tense couple of hours waiting for the special to leave but nothing else happened that night. It did make me understand what was coming in the future, as that night this wasn't Millwall thugs turning out, it was London thugs.

Within a couple of years a loose alliance of various mobs had formed calling itself London United. It consisted mainly of West Ham, Tottenham and Chelsea and sometimes met at a pub in Petticoat Lane. They banded together to attack the Jocks when they came to Wembley and also the big northern clubs, particularly ourselves. Euston was their favourite ambush point.

* * *

NORWICH CITY WAS chiefly memorable for being the first place I saw female skinheads. We took the Norwich end without even seeing a Canaries fan. Then these three girls with cropped hair, braces and boots appeared at the top of the stairs. They were soon getting some stick.

'Dead hard, are you?'

'Where are your lads?'

I'll give them their due, they didn't back down from the verbal, but it didn't take long for things to deteriorate. Little Des and his mates from Salford decided it was time to feel the female and these three birds got ragged all over at the back. Hands went up their jumpers and snapped off their buttons and they were lucky to leave with their clothes still on. Not that they weren't up for it; they were there to make a name for themselves and they knew what would happen.

There was more serious trouble in the ground when we played them again on a Wednesday night in the semi-final of the League Cup. I was at home on the Tuesday night when Jimmy Fitzpatrick and a crowd came from the pub, knocked on the door and said, 'Come on, we're going to Norwich.' It was the wrong time of night to hitchhike but they were pissed and didn't give a fuck. Jimmy and I ended up sleeping in a telephone box on a hill just outside Chesterfield. Mining wagons rolled past all night. We got into a café in Chesterfield in the morning and it then took us all day to get to Norwich. We arrived fifteen minutes before kick-off and I had to tap for money to get in. After the game, because we lost, everyone came out and rampaged, turning cars over and causing as much damage as possible. This was the Red Army in full cry, an unstoppable force. I caught the special back home, and a lot more comfortable it was.

Our away game at Blackpool saw half of Manchester descend on the Lancashire resort for a weekend-long jolly. I vaguely remember getting bladdered and then trying to turn over some jeweller's down a side street. One paper reported that 20,000 were locked out of the ground. That's right, twenty thousand. Scenes like that will never be repeated.

Hull was another place to quake before the boots of the rampaging Red Army. We had a lot of local support in Hull ourselves, and I think the place was a city divided when we arrived. The crowd was 23,000 and probably half supported United. Hull City's South Stand was taken and there was the usual running on the pitch and marauding through the town.

Events were building to a crescendo, and it came that December at Sheffield Wednesday. We took 20,000 in a crowd of 35,000. It was like playing at home. I was in the Leppings Lane End and you could not move. I was gutted that I was in there because I wanted to have a fight. As it happened, I would get into every part of the ground that day.

It first kicked off on our left. A group of 150 Sheff Wed had somehow got in, their lads. They were getting slung all over but tried to keep together as they came further and further down the terrace. The next thing, the whole ground erupted. Once it kicks off, everyone wants to fight.

I ran on the pitch and into the side on my left because there were people in there not wearing red and white. By now it was a mini-riot and the fans were smashing things. Then they brought the horses on the pitch. I next ran right across into the other side. Everyone was on the pitch now. I tried to get back into the Leppings Lane because the group of Wednesday in there had been forced to the bottom. They were smashed but they had made a proper stand. One big black kid was trying to hold them together and was having it good style. In the end the police forced them out of the ground.

Now the horses were trying to get everyone off the pitch. There was no more trouble until Jim Holton broke his leg and then everyone wanted to kill everyone. United eventually took their end; in fact they took the whole ground. The score was 4–4 and by the time Wednesday scored their third they didn't even dare cheer any more.

This was how the *Sheffield Star* reported it:

> Right from the start a steady stream of fans were being taken off the Spion Kop and arrested. Several more were carried out on stretchers by St John Ambulance men.
>
> But the violence really erupted after 30 minutes when for several minutes it looked as if the game might be called off. Dozens of United fans jumped over the barrier at opposite ends of the Leppings Lane End and raced across the pitch to join in. Wednesday goalkeeper Peter Springett fled from his goalmouth as the scarf-waving youngsters charged across his penalty area.
>
> Fighting spread on to the corner of the pitch as scores of police, some on horseback and others wearing white crash helmets, battled with fans. At one time, more than a dozen fans were lying injured on the grass waiting for stretchers to take them to the first aid room.
>
> As the trouble reached its peak, South Yorkshire Chief Constable Mr Philip Knights left his seat in the directors' box to take command. Immediately another 80 policemen were called in to reinforce the 100 already in the ground, and a small knot of Wednesday fans who had been standing on the Kop were evacuated to the safety of the stand.

The day resulted in 106 arrests and fifty-one casualties, and confirmed our status as the pariahs of football. And we revelled in it.

* * *

SOME OF THE best times for football violence come when you are not looking for it, when you are not with all the lads and look like a victim. This is when the other clubs, the bullies, like to seek you out. I have had some of the best rows when not expecting it, games when the lads don't go because they think it will be too quiet.

On one of those days I was taught a lesson I would not forget. Bristol Rovers were regarded as the second team in Bristol. When we played them we had already been to Bristol City that season and had done what came naturally to the Red Army when out in force. We had given Bristol the full treatment: a rampage of destruction and violence. It was burn, destroy, wreck and kill, and City were chased down the road whenever they showed their faces.

> Little Dessie: *We went on the train on Friday night and it was an invasion. Their firm was there but we would have had 8–10,000 fans and there was nothing they could do. People turned up at all hours of the day and night and by 11.30am their town was invaded and occupied. We came to the ground and were jumping on cars, right in front of the police. We smashed everything. People say, 'Yes, United cause havoc, but you have always had the numbers.' But the truth was we might not see Tony and his mob from one match to the next. You got there and did your own thing.*

Our game against Rovers started in fine weather but clouds were building and by the end of the game sleet, rain and snow were lashing our faces. As United came out and made their way to the station, all wet and cold, there was no thought of looking for a fight. I just wanted to get warm and out of the horrible weather. But as we went down the road, a mob of Rovers appeared at the top of one of the side streets. They wanted to know and threw a few rocks at us, so the fight no-one wanted was here. Everyone piled into this narrow side street to have it with them. We had no doubts we'd win the day, but I soon realised we were on a loser as this street was so steep. As we got a short way up, the ones at the front with me and my pals got a shock as Rovers piled down into us.

I couldn't move about and throw punches, as it was difficult to keep your balance and you couldn't kick out for fear of tumbling over. We were falling back to the main road and I took a few punches but Rovers didn't follow up. If they had we'd have swallowed them up from both sides, but they knew this and stood halfway up this incline, taunting us. I was having none of that and started another charge up towards them. We still had quite a few lads but not as many as before and Rovers met us head-on this time. The fighting was fiercer as both sides were intent on holding their ground.

In the end it turned against us. Suddenly my legs were over my head and I was rolling on the floor. I was not the only one. I was quickly up and those of us who were committed to the fight hung in there, giving and taking kicks and punches, but we were getting swamped and no relief was coming. I was kicked in the chest and literally felt a sensation of flying as I went over a car. Some Rovers tried to drag me over the other side of the bonnet and gave me a few stiff digs but I twisted free and virtually rolled down this twat of a hill.

Those of us who'd had it with them were now soaked to the skin and covered in mud off the road. Other United fans at the bottom carried on walking as though nothing was happening, and I couldn't blame them. But even though I had been on the wrong end I had loved every minute of it. I also understood why not everyone had come at them with us the second time; you can't win a fight running up a hill, no matter how many of you there are. Fair play to Rovers, they weren't going to let us win but thanks for the lesson anyway. You'll never learn anything sat on the sidelines.

Oldham was another place where I unexpectedly came a cropper. I went in the Oldham end because that was what you did. About twenty of us were together when a fight started. I expected loads of United to join in but for once they weren't there. From nowhere, I found myself on the floor. I had been volleyed in the belly – and I wasn't even ready for it. Someone must have eyeballed me, come over and planted his boot into my gut. I rolled down the terracing, crawled over the wall and lay in the back of the net as a copper and some first aiders gathered round. I couldn't breathe. I was knackered and, literally, gutted. In the end they carted me off round the side of the pitch until I could breathe again.

Every game had a story that season. At Oxford United I was locked out of the ground. We tried to charge into their end but failed. Loads of United were outside and at the end of the game people were going off their heads, not a riot, just acting up. A big black limo came round the corner with an official flag. We decided it was the mayor's car but for all we knew it could have been a member of the Royal Family. Anyway, it got booted to fuck. The cops tried to nick my mate Rob for vandalising it and he smashed one of them in the face before we escaped into town.

In March 1975 we visited neighbouring Bolton. They hate United. With it being a local fixture, all the firms headed there under their own steam; there was no set plan to meet. Everyone was with their own pals from their own area. We got in Bolton's covered end early, behind the goal. We hung about and gradually Bolton fans filtered in. It wasn't on top but a few kids were giving us verbals. Next thing, my mate was being slung round by one of them and we were having a little go. It stopped and the coppers came in but didn't throw us out. We got a bit more verbal but stood our ground and there were not enough of them to overrun us.

We could see more Reds coming in through our side, in twos, three, fives. All of a sudden they all piled in from the other side, the gangs, and charged into the stand from the left and straight into the Bolton. And who should come surging past but the kid who started the first bit of trouble with us. We were running towards the trouble, Bolton were running away and we were arm-swinging them as they went past. The kid who had given it the big 'un got laid out. Then I butted this kid at the back and he was fucked. A flying headbutt, one of many I have done. He went straight down and then we were all over them. The papers later reported that United 'rampaged through the town and fought on the terraces'. Seventy-four people were ejected from the ground, fifty treated for injuries and forty-six arrested.

*   *   *

WE WERE CROWNED Division Two champions at Notts County on the last day of the season. As chance would have it, our youth leader was entertaining a load of Germans, about fifteen of them. They were archetypal Krauts, stiff as boards with no sense of humour, so in his wisdom he decided to invite them to Nottingham with us lot from Wythenshawe on a coach.

The game was boring, nothing happening, until some United fan decided to climb up a floodlight. The police came on to the terracing and got to the bottom of the stanchion, telling him to come down. This became the entertainment and the focal point for the restless crowd.

'The coppers are going to nick him.'

'Stop them.'

Pushing started, then a few rocks were thrown, then it blew. The terrace crush barriers were wooden and everyone was kicking them, like demolition men, and flinging them at the coppers. Once one group had worked out how to rip the things out, others copied and soon several barriers were being slung about. They got more police in but that made it worse. Now there was a battle on. The lad up the floodlight was not going to get nicked as far as we were concerned, and eventually the coppers had to get out.

It set the scene for the final whistle. Everyone ran round the pitch. Some made it into the directors' box and ripped up the seats. I ran on the grass with my pals and the cops grabbed Russell from Wythenshawe and handcuffed him to the goalposts. He was probably the only person arrested.

Going home was the funniest thing. The Germans, mainly straitlaced students in their mid-twenties, had witnessed this carnage and couldn't believe their eyes. They were in a state of wonderment, and we decided to have a bit of fun with them. I explained what happened when we came home from a match: the older ones had to fight the younger ones. 'Because you're Germans and we're English, you are going to have to fight us,' I said. We made them believe this was a regular routine, just because we wanted an excuse to have a fight with them.

For three-quarters of an hour we knocked fuck out of each other – and they loved it. They were husky lads and they were singing their drinking songs and piling into us in the aisle and on the seats. They had been dead quiet for three days but we sent them home as hooligans.

CHAPTER FIVE

FORTRESS MANCHESTER

MANCHESTER CITY CENTRE was home base for the Red Army. From early on a match-day morning you'd see all the faces that would later be inside and outside the ground. The city centre was where everybody made for first, often even before the pubs opened. It was where I mixed with other gangs from around Manchester and the rest of the country, lads who were United to the core and game for a fight.

The visiting hooligan stood little chance of getting past us. If you didn't get slapped in the morning, you would surely get it after the game, when the whole city centre would still be buzzing and choc-a-block from Piccadilly Railway Station right across to Victoria Station. The only chance you had of negotiating your way in and out without being detected was to avoid being part of a group.

For the likes of Millwall, Cardiff, Chelsea, West Ham, Spurs and other 'notorious' hooligan mobs who revel in their reputations, I have this question: where were you in your hundreds running down Piccadilly and through our city centre? You weren't there – at least not until there was better organisation by the police after they'd been given a kick up the arse by the Government because hooliganism had got completely out of control up and down the country.

In Manchester the situation was simple: you were swamped by the amount of United thugs arriving in town from all over the country. Everyone knew that because of the sheer number of hooligans, the chance of getting nicked was minimal. There were no police escorts to the ground and no proper segregation. Compare what United did when we went away to what all these others did in the days before segregation and effective policing. They never came. They only started arriving after the introduction of segregated sections and big escorts from Warwick Road. In the early Seventies, when the Red Army was flying, you could not get a mob up Warwick Road; it was too packed. It was really rare to see a rival firm. Even when segregation arrived around the mid-Seventies they still wouldn't come. You would get the Scousers; they were the top team, they had to come. But there was no charging up the road together. Cockneys didn't travel north. Let's face it, they couldn't even get it together in their own city to protect Wembley when the Jocks went down for the Home Internationals. If they were hoolies, why didn't they turn out for the Jock invasion?

I'll put into context the problems you faced if you had the bottle in the early Seventies to visit Old Trafford. First was the Cockneys Reds. The London branch of the supporters' club used to hire trains to come to Old Trafford. Gradually hooligans around the Home Counties decided to follow United and the London contingent got the reputation as the Cockney Reds. Imagine two, sometimes three, special trains arriving in Manchester from London for every home game, carrying 5-700 people each, many of them headcases. They were mates through school or work with supporters of London clubs, so we always knew what our rivals in the capital were up to and, more to the point, they knew we knew. We held the fear factor over them.

The Cockney Reds were well organised; they had to be. They had to get to Euston, usually amid other supporters travelling elsewhere, so there were bound to be gangs waiting for them in and around the station. This was a challenge they looked forward to. Equally they knew the real deal would often be waiting on their return home. Arsenal and Spurs were usually the ones who drank in the north London pubs on Saturday evenings, waiting to ambush the Reds coming home. They were fighting before they set off, fighting at the game and fighting again when they got back. These are tales that maybe a Cockney Red will one day tell.

The Cockney Reds not only had numbers, they had some cracking lads who were as game as any. If you looked around you'd see Mick the Con, Banana Bob, Pancho, Robert from Peckham, Roy Downes, Black Sam, all good lads. Some of these I knew well. They mixed with all the Manchester lads and everyone got on. Manchester United was a family, it didn't matter if you were from Blackpool, Birmingham, Corby, Hull, Warrington or Wigan, we were all red, we all loved United and we all knew that everyone else hated us. There was a right bunch of blokes from Warrington, like big Dave, who were always up for it and loved the booze. You had the Telford lot, all the Birmingham lads, all fighters. Everyone was a fighter in the Seventies. And the one thing they had in common with me is they all knew Jeff Lewis, the nutter from Wythenshawe who was my hero.

Another thing about United was that we never went in for any of that National Front stuff. It was a Man City thing, which is odd because their ground was in Moss Side. We have always had black, half-caste and Asian fans. My way of thinking from day one has been, you are a United fan, it doesn't matter where you come from.

Visiting away fans would be sitting on a train for hours, knowing that thousands of drunken thugs were waiting for them, intending to stamp all over their heads – and that's just as they came down the approach from the station. If they did make it to the city centre, we had all the pubs around Piccadilly covered: the Mitre Bar, Yates's Wine Lodge, the Portland Bars and many others. People would know that a train was expected in at 11.30, or whenever, because we talked to each other all week. The Portland was tremendous. You had people upstairs and it would be rock solid downstairs. Everyone was in viewing distance. If something happened on one corner, the others could see or hear it. It was like a trap. We didn't have spotters out in those days because everyone was out anyway. We caused murders, even when there was no-one there. You'd have hundreds walking round town singing, 'War!'

We used to attack pubs because someone *thought* there were away fans in it. We did it for devilment. Someone would shout, 'They're at Piccadilly,' and everyone would charge. The pubs were always full and it only took someone to yell and everyone was out. Myself and lots of other younger lads would roam the streets and stations looking for away fans and if we found any we would challenge them, but they usually knew they had to get off because our older lads would soon be there; some of our lads would already be off to tell the main lads what we had found. What often followed was always funny to us, as we'd end up causing murder in the city centre.

We may have spotted, say, ten Newcastle fans quietly sneaking about looking for a drink where no United fans were. We'd then run around the streets shouting, 'The Geordies are here, there's a hundred drinking in a pub down the road.' From being a quiet afternoon there was suddenly a riot going on. All the United pubs would empty and hundreds from each would charge down the road wanting to be first to smash them in. This had us bouncing up and down laughing but also made us look good, as we ensured we got there with the first group and were at the front. We'd make sure we smashed a window with a brick or a stick. There usually weren't any away fans in the pub at all but from that moment the day had started. Word would now be out that the Geordies, or whoever it was, were here, even though I knew they weren't. Who cared; the mob was now on the hunt. Often we'd do it to relieve the boredom of having little or no opposition, and it was also about getting to know who was who.

One of our finest hours in the city centre was when Wolves played Leeds in an FA Cup semi-final at Maine Road. United were playing at home on the same day and our kick-off was moved forward, presumably to prevent everyone pouring out at the same time. Well if that was the plan it failed spectacularly. After making sure I was at Southern Cemetery with a group from Wythenshawe to brick the visiting coaches as they came up Princess Parkway, I was then out as soon as our game had finished to get back into town. I was not the only one. When Old Trafford emptied every hooligan in the crowd either marched to Piccadilly or got the buses as quickly as they could. You had thousands moving in one direction, with one thought in mind.

The scene at Piccadilly was incredible. I had never seen so many United fans in one place, outside of a football ground. The pavements, roads and side streets were packed. Yet everyone stood still, craning their necks, waiting for the first shout. We remained like that for fifteen minutes. No singing, no noise. It was unreal.

The first buses from Maine Road were spotted pulling up by the court building on Minshull Street. They were Wolves fans, with a police escort. The crowd came to life like a behemoth awoken from deep sleep. Once it started it went on and on. Wolves were getting butchered. We were rampaging, running in circles, like Indians around Custer, chasing them in a huge, swirling mass. They never got back to Piccadilly in a crowd; they were scattered, dispersed, harried and hunted. Their buses were getting wrecked. I've never seen anything like it.

Once everyone had had enough of Wolves, attention turned to Victoria Station, where the Leeds fans would be heading.

'Leeds, it's Leeds now.'

From the Mitre Bar right down to the bottom of Market

Street, the whole area was full of football lads on their way to Victoria to get Leeds. I'll never see anything like it again. You couldn't get to grips with it all. Everyone started running, scarves flying, boots clattering, and there was not a thing the coppers could do.

At the station, however, the police were in a long line barring our way, with cars and vans and dogs. They had bussed the Leeds fans all the way around the centre of town and made sure the specials didn't leave from the front of Victoria but over the bridge. I don't remember actually getting to grips with a mob of Leeds. It didn't matter. We'd made our point. We were invincible in a mob like that.

* * *

A LESS WELL-KNOWN match-day venue was the Golden Gate, by the entrance to Oxford Road station. It was a bit of a secret among hardcore boozers but Reds of a certain age will remember it. It had doormen on and you would get a lot of heavy drinkers from town in there. The Golden Gate was a great point to get the Scousers, because after the game they might get the train from the ground or at Warwick Road and get off at Oxford Road because it was a connecting point for them. Often we would have beaten them to it. Jeff Lewis might be in the Golden Gate with a couple of Cockneys and maybe the older lads going to Warrington or wherever, blokes in their thirties, all drinkers but they knew how to fight. I would go in with them, hanging on Jeff's coat-tail, but there was no-one else my age there. An hour after the match had finished, when the crowds were slowing down, we would pile out onto Oxford Road and maybe find a mob of mickeys walking past, much to their shock.

In the early Seventies, Liverpool did bring big numbers to Manchester on the special and a couple of times charged right through Victoria Station. You couldn't do anything about that; a special in full flow is impossible to stop. But that came to a halt on Boxing Day, 1978, in Piccadilly. Two hundred of us had gathered on Market Street and we knew they'd come off the specials even though we couldn't see them: you could tell by the cops' reaction that they were behind the Arndale somewhere.

We ran down the road and could see them parallel to us, so straight away we whipped down a side street and into the middle of them. We obliterated them, a full special, hundreds of them. They did have an escort but in those days there was one copper per hundred people and we brushed them aside. Once we got into them we split them up and then they were running everywhere. People were on the floor getting leathered while others ran for their skins – and the ones at the front weren't going to turn and help their fallen comrades. We didn't give them a chance to make a stand.

* * *

THERE WAS A game we played early in the morning at Man City fans' expense as they travelled to away games. Sometimes it would start at 9am, depending on where they played that day. We would leave our estates, meet up in the cafes and arcades in and around Piccadilly or Victoria, and lie in wait for the City fans going for their train. We would try to ambush them and give them a kicking before they reached the station. This did not always go to plan. We did not always have an agreed meeting place and sometimes would walk around a corner and bump into some of City's older lads before we'd had time to get together. Then we'd have to get off sharpish. Usually we ended up together, however, and the early morning lads would have it off with them in some side street or chase some of them up to the approach at Piccadilly, where they'd be safe, as many City fans would gather around that area, as if to say, 'This is our territory, so fuck off you little bastards or you'll get it.'

Well, we knew it was them that would get it when they came back at night, as there would be even more of us waiting. This would be achieved by us going around all day winding everyone up, saying the Blues were coming back full of it and had chased us that morning. This really got to most of them, as they were not going to stand for that. So by teatime the lads would be drinking around Piccadilly, waiting for City to come back, and we would be the decoys. We patrolled the streets, checking any sign of arrival, with lads in and out of the station relaying how long before they were due in so we could gather at the bottom of the approach to meet the charge when they came out. City were usually up for it, and our group would front them and take on the ones who came too far in front. Then we would tactically retreat fifty yards or so – and out of the pubs and darkness our hordes would come, hundreds bent on smashing up our hated 'brothers'.

The police, no matter what anyone says, knew what was going to happen and would be chomping at the bit to get stuck in – and that's usually what they did. This would go on for five minutes and then continue for another five or ten minutes down side streets as we ended up in small groups going at it. Sometimes you would find yourself in the wrong group, as you had been fighting that closely, and you'd lose your sense of direction or end up on your arse. If you went on your arse you didn't stay there though; that was the first rule you learnt.

We didn't have it all our own way. Sometimes the Cockneys or some other group of Reds happened to be waltzing through the streets while City waited for their trains to leave, and the City would attack them. All that came out of that was more hatred towards them, as you'd hear stories of blokes with kids being smacked, or women being spat on. But that was City and still is. One thing I can say honestly is that I have never taken a liberty with them, and my pals who are City fans can account for that. Fighting and kicking their arse is a pleasure and there is no animosity from me, as the next day many a time we'll be laughing about it in the pub. Sometimes you would win, sometimes you would lose, but you could have five or six fights in a day.

City did not have our unity. Much of their division stemmed from racial conflict: they had a large number of supporters who got involved in the right-wing politics of the time, but also had a young mob of predominantly black and half-caste youths called the Cool Cats who were making their own name. Naturally they didn't see eye to eye.

George Lyons: *We used to kick off at Maine Road quite a bit. One match we had a bit of a plan: don't get in the ground too early, surprise them. We went in the Kippax, steamed into them. The Cool Cats were there, all coloured lads, and then there was the National Front, and they were fighting among themselves. We had a laugh at that.*

After the match the Cool Cats thought they'd have us. My mate Steve had a knife pulled on him outside this Moss Side shop, so he tipped up the crate of bottles and smashed one of them. They went for him and stabbed him in the hand. I ripped a branch off a tree and whacked one over the head with it. They had a good crew, City, in the early days but there was always too many Reds there. We had a bigger crew and used to organise better. They would come looking for stragglers, try to pick us off one by one, coming into town late. We had to stick together, which we did.

The Cool Cats were led by Donald Francis, one of the up and coming lads from my age group who was moving up to take over from the racist cunts and the older lads. He was obviously going to be one of the figureheads. I would later socialise with Donald. He was a nice lad who I got on with, but on match days all bets were off.

We would also clash with City in nightclubs, though that was more an Eighties thing. In the Seventies there weren't that many places to go; no matter what anyone tells you, the club scene in Manchester was crap. I was going to places like Genevieves in south Manchester when I was sixteen and they were dangerous. That territorial gang thing which had disappeared from the terraces still existed at night. Whenever you got people from different areas there was a problem. You went to the Bierkeller and you would be fighting all night. Pips, which had seven rooms with different music in each and was a trendy club at one time, ended up as another fighting gaff, while Piccadilly bus station was a Wild West show every weekend. Scores would be waiting for the all-night bus and battles always broke out.

Kloisters on a Saturday night was the club for Ancoats and Miles Platting and there would always be United fans in there. It was up the stairs into a dingy room, bit of a balcony, dance floor and bar. At the end of the night people would spill out and there would always be the odd person who had had a dig in the club and wanted revenge. Next thing, the whole of Oxford Road would go up and there'd be all sorts fighting: punks, skinheads, bootboys, rockers, students.

I was got nicked for fighting six weeks out of eight on successive Saturday nights in Manchester. It would kick off and I seemed to always get pulled. In those days they didn't charge you with violent disorder; they would beat your head in, then charge you with drunk and disorderly. You'd get a conditional discharge or a £25 fine; it was easy for the cops and okay for you. On the sixth occasion, the magistrate must have come to the conclusion I was an alcoholic. 'O'Neill, you are only a young lad but you are constantly before this court for drunk and disorderly,' he said sternly. 'I think you need a bit of treatment for your alcoholism.' I nodded contritely but it was all a load of bollocks.

CHAPTER SIX

CLAMPDOWN

THE SUMMER OF our promotion to Division One, we went to Denmark on a pre-season tour. Andy Davies charged us £25 each to go in a minibus and I persuaded the lads to go. He said we were going to stay in a youth hostel in Copenhagen. Off we went, drinking all the way, only for Davies to park the minibus at Dover and say, 'We'll leave that here.' So how were we going to travel on the other side? He wasn't sure. The lads started giving me a bit of stick but we pressed on.

We got on the boat, did a bit of thieving to pay for the drinks, the beer flowed and suddenly there were no problems – but we knew we still had to get to Copenhagen city centre. At some point a bloke on the boat who was driving a Transit van carrying hi-fi equipment agreed to give us a lift. Davies had told him that he was taking a few lads on an exchange trip and his minibus had broken down. We all piled down the stairs to the hold, where the van was, and this poor bloke didn't know what hit him. We jumped in the back and the bloke was ill with it. He only took us so far before completely losing his rag and dumping us at the side of the road, from where we had to hitch.

I was the last to arrive, but our youth hostel was great, with mattresses laid out neatly on the floor. Davies had spun the bollocks somewhat, telling the Danes we were a nice group of lads on a youth exchange arranged through Manchester City Council. We were not quite what they expected – they thought we'd be students, not council estate yobs there to watch United.

One of the lads went out and came back breathless.

'I've just been down to the canal. All these girls came down to go swimming and they all just took their tops off!'

The next day we were all down there in our trunks at 9am sharp, waiting for the girls to show. From then on, it was party time. They loved us and we followed them around like lovestruck sheep. We were copping off because we were different and there was even some shagging going on. It was a different world to the one we knew.

We ended up at Kristiana, the biggest hippy commune in the world. It was an unbelievable place. They had massive barracks for love-ins and their own shacks and workshops in there. It was huge and took ages to walk around. Dogs ran wild and everyone was smoking dope. This was the first time we had seen drugs. I didn't even smoke cigarettes, and it was the same with the other lads. The football got us high.

That trip was the biggest eye-opener I have ever had. It set me on the way, showed me a mentality of freedom. I thought, these people have got it right. They were surviving, doing their own thing, and with not a hint of trouble. You could go anywhere and talk to people. We were mixing with and understanding different cultures and views. It made you relax and enjoy and gave you an incentive to go out there and search. You knew there were better things than your shitty council estate.

Back in Britain for the start of the season, the prospect of the Red Army in Division One was sending the media into a frenzy. The Minister for Sport, Denis Howell, had called for a full report on the behaviour of our fans and there were constant rumours that some sort of government action against us was in the offing. This in turn meant transport staff were loath to work on Saturdays in areas we were travelling to. Typical was one of our first away games that season, at Queens Park Rangers in September 1975. 'Manchester United's Red Army of fans will run into a massive defensive barrier tomorrow in the biggest soccer security operation ever mounted in London,' reported one newspaper. 'Scotland Yard issued a special order of the day to marshal a 250-strong police force.' Tube workers on the Central Line announced a twenty-four-hour strike, busmen refused to run services to the ground between midday and 6pm, and traders in Shepherds Bush market were advised to close and desert their stalls ten minutes before the end of the game.

Other towns were similarly battening down the hatches. At the same time, opposing thugs were gearing up for our visits. Leeds was one of those places where the pre-match hype was justified. We played them that October, and this was how the aftermath was described:

An 'icy grip of fear' hung over Leeds when supporters of Leeds United and Manchester United battled with each other and with the police, a court was told today.

A 'vast, fierce blaze of riot' raged from the city centre to the Elland Road football ground when the two teams met on October 11. There were running battles and pitched battles in the streets. Bricks and bottles were hurled. And it went on from 11am until 6pm.

Mr Ian Pollard, prosecuting, stated this when the first of about 60 supporters of both teams appeared in Leeds magistrates court.

'The battle of Leeds United was fought on the football ground, in the side streets and the broad main streets of the city as warring gangs went on the rampage,' he said. 'Police manpower was stretched to its limit. There were 365 officers on special duty with 84 inside the ground and 281 outside.'

Mr Pollard said: 'They had to deal with battles involving ones and twos, running battles through the streets and pitched battles involving several hundred on each side throwing bricks and stones at each other.

'Frantic pedestrians had to scurry for safety as bricks whizzed about their ears. They heard the sickening thud of boot against body as those involved were either thrown or beaten to the ground and kicked mercilessly. Those on the ground were surrounded by up to ten youths who were just kicking at defenceless bodies.'

In other words it was a typical visit to Yorkshire. We made that long walk to the ground from the station but all the lads were together and we had them before the game. Inside was tremendous, we went down the side and were having them in the ground. But afterwards we came out and in those days you had to go up a slope to a roundabout. They appeared and the only black lad I ever saw with Leeds, a Cockney called Charlie, led them into us wearing a green boilersuit, of all things. We held the line at first but then had to retreat against their numbers and it pretty much continued like that into the city centre. We were getting legged everywhere, because once it starts, you can't stop it. You couldn't tell who was who.

Nothing we had experienced so far, however, matched the hype for our next away game, at Upton Park on October 25. All kind of obstacles were put in the way of the United fans. British Rail refused to run any specials. Day return tickets from Manchester to London were limited to people leaving Piccadilly after 1.30pm and senior citizens on production of a pension book! All police leave was cancelled and a special juvenile bureau was opened to process any youths arrested. Local pubs were not allowed to open until two hours after the final whistle. One top of that, the tubemen refused to operate the District Line beyond

Tower Hill, which was five miles from the ground. Yet bizarrely West Ham refused to segregate the two sets of fans. Maybe they thought no United would turn up. They were wrong.

We took the War Wagon and a van down there on the Friday night. Some of the Danes we had met on our pre-season tour had come over for a reciprocal visit and the birds were over with them. We were staying in a youth club-cum-church hall near Whitechapel in the East End and I went down early to check everything was all right. The rest weren't leaving Manchester until teatime. Their two buses set off and of course they all got pissed up. They stopped at a disco in Walsall and inevitably it went off. One of the lads had an airgun and shot the windows through. The police got them all, the next day's papers declared, 'United Fans Arrested,' and the youth worker was in the shit again. They finally made London at one o'clock.

We were out early on the day of the game but the people I was with were not clued-up. Most were kids off the estate, coming to see the Danish birds, rather than footie lads. We were pissed, a happy-daft bunch, but unbeknown to me the match was promising big-time aggro.

We got to the ground late, to find United's end locked. A BBC TV van was outside and we could hear rumbling inside. The walls, terracing and panelling were being pounded. Shouts and screams, proper aggro sounds, came over the wall and we could hear this commentator describing the scenes in the van. In the end we charged the gate and it moved at the bottom. We pushed it again, the lower hinges went and we managed to raise it to chest height. We gave it one more shove and all dived in before it swung back down.

We looked up the steps to see United fans on the South Bank staring down at us, with very tense expressions. West Ham had half the end and had been coming from behind and steaming United, who were hanging on. Every ruffian in the East End was out for this one. The United fans had heard us kicking in the gate and were worried it was yet another West Ham kamikaze assault. That's how bad it was inside.

We got onto a cramped corner of the terrace and it was heavy. If it hadn't been for the police, West Ham would have destroyed us. They were even coming through the police at certain stages and United were fighting back for dear life. The crush got really bad and straight members began to climb onto the pitch near the corner flag for safety. I wasn't having it, so this big-titted Danish bird and I went round and got into the side. The game was held up for nineteen minutes to clear fans off the pitch.

West Ham were out for blood that day. It was a shock to me, because they had never come to Old Trafford. 'The Day The Terrace Terrors Were Hunted Like Animals And *Hammered!*' declared the London edition of the *Sun*. They claimed West Ham had 'routed' the Red Army. Well they were certainly out in force that day, and the following season United fans were banned from going back there. The FA held an inquiry into what happened, with most of the blame being put on the West Ham mob – which made a change.

* * *

UP TO THE start of United going back into the First Division, our travels up and down the country had been nothing but anarchy. It couldn't last. There was now a large group of United fans who stopped wearing colours at matches, as it was a way to infiltrate the opposition without the police clicking on. All they'd ever ask you was where you were from, so if it was Scousers you were playing, out came the 'Liverpool, la.' Sometimes you came unstuck if the police knew your face and even the strongest protest in a fake accent wouldn't help, but usually you could get in most ends without difficulty.

The Government were compelled to act, as hooliganism was

seen as a wide and spreading social problem – and the root cause was United. The authorities realised that much of what was happening was actually criminal activity under the guise of football hooliganism. This wasn't just a United thing; it was also pioneered by those down the road in Merseydive. Shops were being looted, jewellers were targeted, and many a time the mob would be diverted by the shout of some crafty bastards who had spotted an earner. It was easy to divert people when they were in full cry and hyped up. The Government decided to stem this, but anyone who knows the score will tell you that things only got better for the grafters, as the travel scene abroad opened up. Lads began to go thieving in the summer, and the French, Germans and Scandics didn't know what had hit them.

One of the first ventures was a pre-season to Belgium, when coachloads left Chorlton Street station for Dover and then went over to Ostend. All the lads were at it and went through that place like a plague. A lot of my generation would become thieves and criminals, initially through doing jewellery store windows and clothes shops on match days. I rarely participated in that. My mentality was trouble: fighting, fighting, fighting. Oh, and watching the match for ninety minutes.

Racism was also becoming an issue. The National Front and the British Movement were recruiting thugs from the terraces for their marches and propaganda. As more people bought television sets, the appetite for news and sensationalism grew, while newspapermen were running around every weekend trying to tap into the market of the football thug. They easily came into contact with racists willing to spout out their vile crap, and the media fuelled it.

Other youths drawn to football were looking for excitement they didn't find in their daily lives. This generation were breaking away from the idea of going to work with little to show for it. The working-class man was not seeing rewards for his hard labour. All he could see through the media was the rich getting richer and looking down on hard work. Whether it was the right perception I don't know, but that is how people felt. So again agitators spouting about how society was keeping the working man down found a ready audience among the thugs.

People look back at the Sixties and early Seventies and say it was full of excitement and peace and that the future looked rosy. Well, not if you came from my background. What I remember seeing on TV was a society in rebellion and a Government with its head in the sand. As children we saw news reports of mods and rockers fighting at seaside resorts on bank holidays and you wished you were there as it looked like fun, something that you thought was normal behaviour for teenagers. Through the Sixties we saw the race riots in American cities and the student riots in Paris in 1968. The Vietnam War fed us uncensored images of killing day in day, day out, something that had never happened before. How could people not be affected by this?

In the Seventies we lived through constant industrial unrest, a miners' strike that brought down a government, power cuts and the three-day week. We watched footage of riots in Northern Ireland, where huge mobs fought, threw petrol bombs, burned buses, looted and left swathes of destruction. We saw poorly-prepared police powerless to protect themselves, something we exploited ourselves on the terraces and in the streets.

I never saw myself as a radical in any way, I just looked at my surroundings and thought, fuck this, there's no way I'm going to listen to this bullshit about work and saving up for retirement, what a joke that is. Ask the millions of pensioners who struggle to survive if it was worth scrimping and saving only to end up without even a decent pension for most to live on. I decided that no way was I working in a dead-end job to be told what to do, to earn money for the political classes and get fuck all myself and have no life. I had no money even for a holiday – the best I could do was a day out to Blackpool. Don't do what the Government tells you because they are all self-serving bastards.

Football was going to be my life and anything that came with it I would grab; it didn't matter if it was money from the turnstiles or knocking out the programme seller, this was how I would survive. And I would have a great time doing it. No-one was going to change me. I decided that life was for now, not when you're old. I made my choice and have never regretted it.

* * *

MY REPUTATION HAD spread further than I thought. In 1976, I sat in the Old Trafford boardroom with the Labour Sports Minister, Denis Howell, and club chairman Martin Edwards at a meeting to discuss football hooliganism. I had been running violent trips, had been in the newspapers and was recognised as a leader. So when Howell came to Old Trafford on the day of a game against Liverpool, I was invited along with social worker Andy Davies. Howell wanted my opinion and I told him how groups would travel and organise and whatever. Edwards was very aloof and didn't give a fuck.

I knew it was all bullshit but I went along for the ride. We had cups of tea and biscuits, all very polite, and then at 1.30pm I came out to the usual scenes of madness. I got to the top of Warwick Road and the whole street and all around the ground erupted because the Scousers had made a good move. They had got off their train at Oxford Road and had then caught one of those three-carriage local trains – and we could see it coming. However, they didn't want to get off because they had no police with them and they knew what would happen if they weren't protected. As they got nearer, something had to be done, so they pulled the cord on the far side of the bridge. There were thousands of us, not just hardcore lads but loads of our barmy army, or barmies as we called them. I looked over the bridge and saw the Scousers piling out of the train doors. We could see them on the track, about 200 of them, the boys.

We knew they had to go through the platform and we tried to get underneath and through the turnstiles at them. Rocks flew both ways and from the bridge. The police were in the middle with both sides screaming blue murder. And who was sat in the boardroom overlooking the start of this riot? My new pals, Howell and Edwards.

In the end the police made a gap in the tunnel by the South Stand and we were having the Liverpool as soon as they came into the open. It was like a wave going back and forth. The Scousers were penned together with their hands up by their faces for protection and we battered into them. They couldn't fight back because they were so pressed together – but at least they had come. Heaps of them were getting thumped and stamped and they were keeping hold of each other so they wouldn't get dragged out of the pack.

I was later invited to Denis Howell's constituency offices in Birmingham. His private secretary was there, the full works. I had never seen anything so plush: thick leather chairs, a huge drinks cabinet, a white carpet that looked like the back of a polar bear. I reclined in one of his comfy chairs and drank his brandy while discussing ways of dealing with the curse of the Red Army and how it could be controlled. We sat and talked and then I came out with the social worker and we discussed it and I said, 'They don't give a fuck.' So I ignored trying to be a goodie-goodie organiser in the way they wanted. But then the club never gave anything to the fans. Andy Davies also arranged for me to go to Aston University and do a talk for two hours to undergraduate students. I got a standing ovation.

I was self-educated in life. I wanted to be involved in the club as a fan, not as a hooligan. I wanted it to be part of my family, but the club alienated the fans. They wouldn't bring them in. I was left with what I had, which was the street. I turned my back on the official side of things. They didn't want us at away games, even though the crowd could turn a game and lift the players.

* * *

A LOT OF the lads had been arrested at football – some of them many times – but I had so far escaped. My time came at Arsenal, around 1976. It was on Euston Road and we were chasing them up the road. They had come off Euston Square and after a bit of a scuffle we legged them. I chinned one and a copper got on my case but couldn't catch me. We got back to Euston and the copper was on the stairs, waiting. As we filtered back, he grabbed me. He put my arm up my back, slapped me, and I ended up at Clerkenwell Magistrates Court.

The copper told the court he had arrested me at a certain time. Unfortunately for him, just before I was nicked I had been talking to Chris Lightbown, a freelance reporter I'd got to know who had just got off a train from Liverpool. The cop's story of my time of arrest did not tally with the time Lightbown's train came in – it was twenty minutes out. So when Lightbown turned up at court and testified on my behalf, I got a not guilty. We went straight to the pub over the road to celebrate.

The cops in the Seventies were a different breed. In the good old days they joined in and whacked anybody. If they did nick you, you got a poxy charge. These days they hunt you to give you a serious charge, but one hand doesn't know what the other is doing.

Lightbown later came with us on the train to Leeds and wrote a story about me in the Sunday Times. He called us the 'outsiders' because we were not part of the official trips organised by 30,000-member supporters' club. Instead we made our own travel and ticket arrangements.

Around about this time I also appeared in the *Manchester Evening News*:

Gang who reformed
face a bus ban

A youth worker is being banned from using an official mini-bus to take a gang of Manchester United supporters to away matches.

Mr Andy Davies has been using the bus with the gang – they call themselves the Crossacres Reds – for 18 months. But the city education committee has decided to forbid its use following an incident last November in which youths were questioned by police in Walsall.

Mr Davies, aged 36, who does his job as a detached youth worker from the former police house he owns in Solway Road, Wythenshawe, also faces an interview with the chairman of the community education sub-committee.

Mr Davies, whose job is to contact youngsters who would not use youth clubs, would not comment today on the proposed ban. But it was attacked by 17-year-old Tony O'Neill, of Nuffield Road, Wythenshawe, leader of the Crossacres Reds.

He said: 'Almost all the lads in this gang have convictions for offences like fighting, damage and threatening behaviour at football matches but since we asked Andy to organise trips to away matches 18 months ago there has been a big change.

'The amount of trouble has gone down steadily and now we are a well-behaved gang who do not get into trouble. Andy pointed out which way we should go.'

The Walsall incident took place when the gang were on their way to London for a game against

Arsenal. They met a group of Walsall supporters at a disco and had what Tony called 'a great night with them with no trouble at all.' But later they were taken to a police station because an air pistol was found in the Minivan.

Tony said: 'We had done nothing wrong so they could not charge us. The pistol was returned and we have now banned the lad who had it from going to matches with us.'

I could spin a yarn when need be! In the end the War Wagon went up in flames. I was at my house when Steven Hesford and Willie Farrell knocked on my door one night and said a thieving gang of Man City urchins from Benchill had used it to go to West Ham. As far as we were concerned it was our War Wagon; we were certainly not having City fans using it. It had been desecrated.

'What are we going to do?' they asked.

'Go and burn the fucking thing,' I said. 'No-one is using it now.'

It didn't matter to me by then because I had moved on and was hiring coaches or travelling on service trains. We had drifted away from the War Wagon and certain members of our Wythenshawe gang had found girls and football wasn't of the same interest to them any more. The War Wagon mysteriously caught fire outside Davies's house. I was nearly eighteen and it was embarrassing to be around him then anyway.

* * *

THE RED ARMY had moved on from its domination of the Second Division – but at a price. We had been singled out by the Government, which put pressure on the Football Association to deal with the crisis – and in the early to mid-Seventies it was a crisis for law and order up and down the country. The authorities thought they could bring in measures to control us, but all they did was bring us closer together as a fighting unit. In a sense the Government did us a favour. Grounds started erecting fences, but crap fences. We were subject to all-ticket restrictions which saw us penned into newly constructed areas at away grounds which accommodated only 3–4,000 away fans. This distilled us to a hard core, not an army anymore. They also, inadvertently, created the ticket tout. We would always find a way to get in.

So the war between the Government and the hooligan gangs was on. Mobs became more organised and even more focussed. All that had gone before with the Red Army – wearing your colours, pitch invasions, mass wrecking and large-scale attacks on the home end – was fading, to be replaced by streamlined mobs who wanted to seek out and destroy the mob from the other side. It had all been a learning curve, even the setbacks when the opposition had turned us over. Now all over the country people were waiting for us, so they could be the ones to say they saw off Tommy Doc's Red Army. We had to take it to a new level. It was graduation time.

CHAPTER SEVEN

RED ARMY LEADER

WHEN WE WERE young we loved to stir up trouble. Occasionally we would travel by service train, because the specials often arrived too late for us to cause any mischief. You might have 250–350 on the service for the odd game, split into the youngsters and the older heads. So one day, coming back from a game at Derby, all us young lads took on the old 'uns in an impromptu battle. The older blokes liked kicking our heads in, to be honest. It began with a bit of verbal, then Eddie Beef from Collyhurst or one of the other livewires started acting up, the first lightbulb was unscrewed and hit someone on the head, then it was:

'Come on then, do you want it?'

It properly kicked off in the middle of this long train, with us trying to hold one side and them the other. In those days British Rail had fire axes on the trains, and Harry the Dog grabbed one and whacked me over the shoulder with it. Other people were getting fire extinguishers bounced off their heads, all in fun you understand.

All us youngsters ended up jammed in the last carriage. There was nothing left of the train: no light bulbs, no windows, no seats, it was an empty shell. There were some injuries as well, people with cut heads, and Harry was still waving the axe about. We pulled in and I think we were all relieved to be at Piccadilly. We teamed up again and charged through town looking for City. After that the young versus old battles were a regular feature.

I had been known for a while as the leader of some of the younger lads, but now I was beginning to get full recognition from the top boys. For every lad who has ever become a terrace leader, there is a turning point, a moment when you make that step up. Mine came at Middlesbrough, when I was seventeen years old.

We went up to Ayresome Park in December 1975 on the train. I knew nothing about the place but found out that day how tough it was. United had caused havoc there in the early Seventies and we were guaranteed a hot reception. We had to go through town before the game and they were all in the streets and shops. They tried to stand their ground but we went through them.

I had taken Clint Turner to the game, who was even younger than me. Clint, who's dead now, rest his soul, was a sound lad. He and I came out of the ground and into all the side streets. We walked straight ahead at first, then went left and right, zigzagging through the streets. As we turned yet another corner, we heard the noise of battle, and in front of us saw Boro running at a small group of United.

One of the Reds was Dave Willis, a hard case from the north Manchester crowd, who stood to have it. Unfortunately his mates didn't, and he was left on his own. He could have tried to get away, but being the man he was Willis fronted them on his own.

'There's Dave Willis,' I said to Clint. 'Fucking hell.'

The Boro were on him, punching and kicking. Dave fought to stay on his feet, knowing that if he went down he'd be stomped to pieces, but the odds were hopeless. As if with one mind, Clint and I ran in and jumped on the backs of two of his attackers. We lashed out, connecting with wild punches, and they backed off momentarily, not knowing how many of us there were. That gave a few seconds' respite. We grabbed Willis.

'Dave, run!'

The three of us ran like hell. We made it back to the station where loads of United were waiting. Once we were safely on the special, Willis went absolutely mental at the lads that had left him. He ranted up and down the carriage, pointing to me and Clint.

'These fucking young lads, they backed me up and you fuckers left me. You fucking left me. And these are only kids.'

He held a kangaroo court in the carriage, and went through the mob identifying everyone who had fucked off and left him. It was a major incident within the firm; he even ended up punching one of the lads. Willis was judge, jury and executioner. It was harsh but absolutely necessary to ensure that in future no-one fucked off and left one of the lads at the mercy of a mob. It was the start of us getting together as a proper hooligan firm, separate from the mass of the Red Army. Even though some of us had left school only a year earlier, this was the coming of age: we were grown up now and the rule was that you were not allowed to abandon anyone in the shit.

I don't think after that the firm ever left anyone.

My actions at Boro allowed me to mix and be accepted by all the lads as someone who wouldn't let you down. I already knew most of the main lads, but from then on my position was secure. They all knew: 'O'Neill won't let you down.' I wouldn't bottle it and run.

But there was never a lot of back-patting and congratulations in our firm, sit down and discuss things, well done, et cetera. If someone turned round and said, 'Wow, I saw you doing such and such,' then what were they doing? They must have been watching instead of getting stuck in.

All my life I've never been one at the back. I have got loads of energy; I can't saunter. It was impossible for me not to be at the front, and psychologically I have to be there because I have to be able to work out if it's coming on top, how to hold it, how to back them off, and so on. I'm not putting my life in the hands of someone else. It has been once or twice, maybe more, but I have always tried to make sure that no-one tells me how to put my life in danger.

A young crew was developing and eventually someone had to take charge. They didn't have a number one leader: I was one of a handful of main heads that were reliable. Then it got to the point: here we go. People trust me and that is where the respect comes from. They know that if I am putting them in that situation I will get stuck in. I won't put them in danger and not go in myself. If I'm in charge people often wait to see how I react. If I believe it is on top they wait until I tell them, 'Hang back,' or whatever. In a tight spot I will tell them, 'Walk slowly, get together.' Then I'm in – and I expect the people with me to follow without me having to look behind, worrying. If I go in and get done and they leave me, they know the first thing I will say to them afterwards is, 'Where the fuck were you? I went in, why didn't you?' But I never got done in, not properly put down on the deck and kicked to fuck, because the people behind me understood.

It got more and more streamlined after the year we were relegated. A few main faces pulled it together. In 1973–4 it was still groups from different places even though they were together. There were no main leaders. Everyone respected everyone and no-one dominated. As these groups came to trust each other, having shared some hairy situations, they coalesced into a genuine Manchester firm. Then one or two figureheads emerged who were respected because they had proven themselves as leaders and as fighters. I had proven that I would be there and get stuck in. I was always there.

We had always used service trains occasionally, but now

because of the problems with the specials and also their timing, we began to use them more. We wanted to get in that town for pub opening or before the trouble started, to make a few quid. For some reason the police didn't get on the service trains so you had freedom. Plus no-one ever paid.

We would discuss it in the pubs or on the streets the week before. It was usually obvious which one you wanted – if a train got you in at 10.30 or 10.45 then that was the one. We wanted to enjoy the full day.

* * *

THE BEGINNING OF that season saw tremendous battles at away grounds, as we now stuck together at the final whistle and charged out in bulk to take it to whoever was there. The police responded by sometimes locking the gates and keeping you in for twenty minutes to allow the home fans to disperse. This was at times a relief, as it gave you more time to arrange the lads at the front, something which that year gave us a right result at Liverpool, our sworn enemies for life.

Previously at Liverpool, United had held their own before the game but it was potluck whether you got back to Lime Street unscathed or not, as the vermin would be on every corner and you knew some were carrying carpet knives. To stand and have it in those circumstances was rarely an option. You would always hear of tales of people walking to their cars or coaches being cut up, ordinary supporters. It didn't matter to the vermin, that was their way. But the tables had started to turn because although they would pen us into a corner in the Anfield Road End – how nobody ever got squashed to death is a miracle – it brought the best out in us. We used to go berserk in there and couldn't wait to get out, building ourselves into a frenzy.

Ten minutes after the whistle, out we came and were forced right towards the Arkles pub. Across the road were buses to collect those going to the train station. Scousers were everywhere in the side streets, on the roads, near the buses, thinking they would pick us off. What a shock they got. We smashed into the ones on the corners and then continued towards the Arkles, with the Scousers bouncing towards us. With a full war cry, we ran at them, all the lads together. No one stood off, no one bottled it, we were into them as one, chasing them all over and smashing them up and down the street, into the big car park at one point and back out on the opposite side to head back towards the coaches and buses. It was pure violence for fifteen minutes.

The police could not keep us apart and resorted to doing what comes naturally to the Scouse copper: lashing out with their truncheons and those long sticks they had. What we didn't hear that night was the usual Scouse bizzie response to a United fan caught in a sticky situation: 'Well you shouldn't have come, so fuck off.' Now the boot was on the other foot. And to all those useless Merseyside dibble who let away fans get butchered on their patch, I take great delight in having created pure fucking aggro for you lot for thirty years and having made your lives a misery. You reap what you sow. Not once did you bother when someone was slashed or beaten up, so when you copped it from that day on, God it was good. Liverpool was now a level playing field and the Scousers knew it.

* * *

IN THE SUCCESS-STARVED Seventies, our FA Cup semi-final against Derby County at Hillsborough was a major event. We weren't even favourites but Tommy Doc had begun to pull together an exciting team of flying wingers and skilful ballplayers. The ground was absolutely Man United, red and white everywhere. I was in the Derby section and that was half United. This had occurred through the ticketing system designed to keep us out. In fact I don't even remember having a ticket for the game.

I was in the middle of the open end. Derby's lads were there and I was with a couple of lads but not the main ones usually associated with fighting. This bald-headed Derby fan and I went at it, two or three times. I couldn't understand how we were stood next to them with no police down the middle and there was no fighting. We tossed a few verbals back and forth so I went and got myself involved and smashed this baldy in the face. I had to start it because that was what we wanted; I wasn't concentrating on the game. The scuffle was just centred in the middle and didn't spread; it wasn't a fight where we were trying to beat them up and get them out of the end. I was fighting away and people were trying to whack me and it seemed as though just a few were involved. Then it stopped and we all just stood in the same positions we had started. I was baffled. It was like no-one wanted to know.

A bit more verbal went on and this happened a few times and the same few people scuffled again. This Derby fan, who was much older than me, I ended up having three fights with him, which got a bit boring. There was no excitement and in the end we both gave up. We both stood our ground but there was nothing more to do. I thought it would spark a riot and on any other day it would have, yet even when they scored the goals there was no trouble. But it was fantastic that we won.

Events outside, however, showed that old habits die hard:

POLICE injured, pubs wrecked, homes vandalised, and 93 arrests . . . Manchester United may have covered themselves in glory at Sheffield on Saturday, but for some of their fans there was only disgrace.

In a two-hour orgy of violence, a screaming mob of 3,000 Reds' fans:

ATTACKED police, putting three in hospital. One

was beaten to the ground and kicked in the face. His wounds needed six stitches.

SMASHED up two pubs and robbed an off-licence and badly beat up a barman steward.

VANDALISED private houses near the ground – many of which had been boarded up in fear of what was to come. Windows were smashed, fences uprooted and washing stolen from lines.

OVERTURNED 10 cars parked near the ground, causing thousands of pounds worth of damage. Other cars were kicked, scratched and had their tyres punctured.

TRIED to charge down one gate to the ground, but were beaten off by police.

FOUGHT several pitched battles with Derby fans, from which most of the 93 arrests stemmed.

A Sheffield police spokesman said today: 'They were even scrapping Sheffield United fans leaving the city to go to a match at Norwich!'

The main thing was that we won and were on our way to Wembley. *Que sera, sera*, and all that. Our opponents were Southampton, a team without much of a hooligan reputation. Well let me tell you, that is one tough place, a dockers' area and one of those towns where a visit from Man United was a call to arms for every lunatic from miles around.

I don't remember much, if any, trouble at the final – which, of course, we managed to lose. It was dead boring because the crowd was all United. My only bit of excitement was robbing a Cockney tout outside who wanted £25 for a ticket, which was a week's wage then. He was relieved of tickets which got us into their end, but it was half United in there anyway. The game was chiefly notable for the amount of snide tickets being kited around by Scousers. They were like bus tickets in those days and the mickeys had cottoned on to it and run off batches of fakes.

On visits to Southampton itself, I saw plenty of action. On one occasion quite a lot of us got into their open end early in the day. At the time we didn't rate them. I saw some Cockney Reds in there and expected more and more United to come in to try to completely take the end. We were at the top left and had quite a big space, but as kick-off drew nearer and more Saints came in the tide turned against us. We tried to push them back but were getting pushed and kicked into the corner. By the time kick-off came we were hanging on for dear life to stay in there. By just after half-time we were all out of there. They had done us and forced us out, big blokes as well. They got stuck into us and there was a battle royal downstairs at half-time. That sorted it out because we couldn't get back on the terracing after that.

The next time we went there, for a cup game, there was heavy fighting outside before the match. There was no thought of taking their end that day, but when we lost the match our fans went mad. We knew this was going to be a proper fight, not a hooligan rampage. They seemed a lot older than us and not as daft. Anyway we piled around to their end to have it. It was a long way to go without having a proper fight, so we had to do it. I came round the corner and they were coming down and having it proper. The police steamed in at some point and Eric Hamnett from Wythenshawe, who already had a string of previous from the footie, later got eighteen months for it, which was a lot at the time.

Eric was with me a couple of years later when I was finally caught out by the cops. We had played Aston Villa in February 1976. There'd been a rampage after the game – in one street near the ground a quarter of all the houses had their windows put through and people had tried to set fire to parked cars. A coachload of us stopped on the way back at this quiet pub called the Shakespeare in Newcastle under Lyme. I was with ten or twelve of my mates along with forty others who were all from Wythenshawe and were some of the hardest lads of their day. They were no mugs.

As usual the question came up:

'Where are you from?'

'Manchester.'

'Yeah?'

'Yeah, we're United fans.'

You can picture it, some cunt chatting along as though he's your mate but you know what he's up to. Off he goes but you just know he's coming back with his pals. And in they came dead on nine o'clock, charging through the pub and round to the vault, Stoke City fans thinking they were going to give it us. Well, we hadn't been sat there twiddling our thumbs: we'd all drunk as much as we could and then stacked the empties on the tables and window sills.

They came through the vault door and, smash, they were met with everything. As those who came through first tried to turn to get back they were now falling over the others who were trying to get in. We just gave them everything: pool balls, the odd table smashing on them, pool cues to the back of the head and lots of pint glasses. All they could do was scramble back out the way they had come. As we regrouped in the vault, I was greeted by the sight of Rob Slater smashing everything behind the bar with a pool cue. I don't know why, maybe it was his way of saying don't fuck with us.

We were all high with adrenalin but knew we still had to go out into the street, and we had no idea how many were waiting. A couple of minutes later when we were ready, we went to face more. Two steps outside and I was in a headlock, courtesy of a police officer. The street was full of dibble and eleven of us were arrested.

This was what the local newspaper reported:

'The fans came in for a drink and all of a sudden someone shouted, "United, United" and the whole place just blew up,' said the manager, Mr Edwin Clunn.

'They were throwing tables, glasses and chairs. They were fighting with everything they could lay their hands on.

'They just turned on my regulars and then they ran out. There was nothing they could do but bolt the doors behind them.'

One youth had 33 stitches in head wounds. Another was treated for cut wrists.

Several of us ended up in court. I pleaded guilty while the others not guilty. That fight got me four months in Wellington House, a detention centre in Stoke, while the rest got between six and eighteen months.

Wellington House was a violent place and the screws were sadistic. I spent the summer of 1976 there, one of the hottest on record. Two things stick in my memory. One was watching the footie results in the telly room at the start of the following season: the Baseball Ground comes on and I see Chelsea and Derby rioting on the pitch. I jumped up and started shouting encouragement at the screen – that's how much of a thug I had become. From nowhere a screw smashed his fist into the side of my face, then dragged me off, giving me the odd kick in the stomach before throwing me back in my dorm. That may sound brutal but it was nothing compared to what other lads got back in the Seventies.

The other thing I remember is getting released. I was eighteen when I came out and they released me as fit as a fiddle, which was just what I needed for the start of the new season. We had spent every day, every hour exercising non-stop. They thought it would cure you but like anything you adapt. The treatment they dished out only made me more angry – particularly as my spell inside also jeopardised my job as a youth worker – so when I came out I was as fit as a boxer and full of fury. Match day could not come quickly enough.

* * *

FENCES WERE GOING up in grounds around the country and fans at many grounds were now being penned in. At Old Trafford, we now had the seats of K Stand above the Scoreboard End, and to the left the fearsome Scoreboard Paddock, which contained nothing but big, drunken nutters. The 'lads' now mainly sat in K and B Stands, two areas which were advantageous as we could legitimately hang about outside the entrances, with no hassle from the police, until the away fans arrived. Yes, away fans were showing up at Old Trafford, not in their thousands yet but sometimes enough for us to attack as they were escorted to the turnstiles. It did not help the police that United also opened the Supporters' Travel Club right next to the away turnstiles, so we could pretend to queue up there as the escorts were brought to the ground.

As the police brought the escort closer you would get one group trying to disrupt it from one angle, then other groups were coming from their set places as and when the police left their lines to repel the first attack. This would leave room elsewhere for the lads to move in and mingle with the opposition, causing confusion. More often than not the away fans would panic as we gave out slaps, which resulted in them trying to run one way or another, which usually meant straight into another slap.

The only time early on at football I saw this happen and got a slap myself was before a game at Newcastle. We got off the football special to face a proper mad scene walking to the ground. Thousands of Geordies filled the streets, battling to

get at us from every angle. It seemed as though the whole city
had turned out. The police kept the majority at bay but we
managed to have it a few times with some large groups. I
knew, however, things would deteriorate as we neared the
ground. There was no holding back what felt like the whole
Geordie nation. They knew our lads were there and they were
after revenge for humiliations suffered at Old Trafford and
around Victoria Railway Station in Manchester.

The Geordies, we felt, did not have the football firm mentality.
They would come to Old Trafford and fight but never as a big
unit, always in small groups on coaches or in vans, so they often
copped for it. They were hardcases in the main – in fact every
one seemed to be a raving lunatic – but weren't organised. They
acted as a crowd without a focal point. This gave better-organised
firms an advantage over them, but on this day their sheer
numbers and their burning desire for vengeance made up for any
shortcomings. We faced a hiding.

We reached the ground with a few cut heads from bottles
and bricks but still together, which was the main thing. The
Geordies pressed all around the cordon. A few mingled in with
us and we slapped one or two but they were suicidal and not
even the coppers were able to drag them away. The scene was
utter anarchy and after a few minutes, with even the coppers on
horses losing the battle to keep them back, we tried to gain
entry to the ground before we lost it.

It was too late. We had our backs to the wall and the Geordies
were now running into us. It became a desperate battle to hold
it together. Everybody was giving and taking punches and the
roar of Geordies baying for blood was deafening. Yet it was a
great feeling. I punched someone who was punching a United
lad while at the same time someone else was punching me. In
the excitement you don't feel it until afterwards and then there's
only one cure – a few pints.

The police restored order after a few minutes but it had

stretched them to their limits. They had battled as hard as any of us and I for one was glad on this occasion that they were there. And this was only the beginning. I knew from bitter experience how bad it could be inside St James's.

* * *

MY FIRST VISIT to Newcastle had been a few years earlier and had been a real eye-opener. It saw our Jeff Lewis brought to his knees, and that was no easy feat. I had hitchhiked alone the night before and holed up in a dingy café until I saw some Reds arrive. I followed them to a pub and found Jeff, Pancho and a few other lads in their thirties. It was pretty moody in and around the boozer but things stayed calm. I made my way to the ground early so I could cadge a few quid and had no problems, but I knew it would be bad inside the ground, as you could see into the back of the open stand where United were supposed to be and you knew it was mixed. In fact at that early hour it looked as though it was all Geordies; instead of waiting they had got in the ground early and positioned themselves nicely in and around where we would gather, behind the goal. Yours truly was a bit tricky himself in those days and realised it was observation time – time to learn. And learn I did.

Some of Jeff Lewis's group eventually made it to the ground – and some did not. Jeff himself was hospitalised after being hit with an iron bar. He had led the lads into the Geordies on the way to the ground, heavily outnumbered but with little choice. Someone smashed Jeff over the head and an ambulance took him to hospital for stitches.

It took more than that to keep Jeff Lewis down and at half-time he arrived, his head swathed in bandages. He must have wondered where everyone was, as he had missed a classic assault from the top of the terracing by the Geordies. They gathered high up and then piled into United behind the goal. I witnessed this from beside the floodlights and then saw my first pitch invasion by the home fans at an away ground. Thousands, or so it seemed to me, charged across the pitch and were jumping into United's so-called end; I say so-called because we barely had possession of it. They had thousands on the pitch and were like an imitation of us at our worst. Resistance from the Red Army didn't last long, as the situation was hopeless. Those United fans who entered the ground late mingled in and kept quiet. Only a few stood together, isolated by the police, and they too were muted.

Afterwards I went to the station to jib the train. Geordies were running everywhere trying to find United fans. I was on my own and relatively inconspicuous but I was getting paranoid; so much so that I ran round a corner into a car park and hid underneath a car. I didn't even want to look at a Geordie and give myself away by appearing nervous; they were hunting United everywhere. Plus they were all in black and white, and I wasn't.

After ten minutes I got up and made my way to the station. I found about 180 United, many of them battered and bruised. The coppers took us on to the platform, hiding us away from the main station. On the other side of the tracks was a kid with a Glasgow Rangers shirt on, for some reason, giving it the big one. A United fan went down and round and we could see him creeping up on this mouthy guy in the Rangers shirt. We went quiet as the lad crept up behind him, walloped him from the side and sparkled him on the floor. We all jumped up and cheered; it was the result of the afternoon, because it had been on top all day.

* * *

THE DIFFERENCE NOW was there was segregation in the ground. The end behind the goal was divided by a large metal barrier down the middle and also at the back of the stand. Once we were all in together we could sort out what had gone on and organise what to do after the game. Not only had we got to the ground, we had given out a fair few digs to the Geordies and survived, which in those days was a victory in itself.

Nothing much happened for the first thirty minutes of the game, but as half-time approached people on both sides were giving each other abuse, often followed by a few bricks and the inevitable fan knocked out and carried off bleeding from a head wound. This was the time for all the lads to regroup at the back of the stands where the stairs, toilets and refreshments were, not that the refreshments ever lasted long as the tills were usually robbed and the kiosks smashed up. The motto back then was eat first, then get your money back.

We went down the back, acting up, and with the Geordies also going on with themselves you knew it was going to go off. The barrier separating us was built so elephants couldn't get through it, but you can count on the Geordies to have a go. They were pushing and shoving and trying to drag it down, and it looked like they were succeeding. They egged each other on as I took my position on the stairway, where we were now packed like sardines. At the bottom all the lads had moved back, then all of a sudden, 'Smash it down!' and in the Geordies came – but only thirty to forty, who literally fell into our section of the stairs. Our lads at the bottom pounced and we bounced them off the floor and the toilet walls. We showed no mercy, as there were hundreds behind them, and they lost the momentum and never followed up. The police, now reinforced, came in whacking and forced both sides back up into the terracing. It was a nice little result and we were bouncing about with glee. Those who knew the score realised that if the Geordies had followed up when the barrier went down, things might have been different. I savoured the moment.

If anyone thought that was the end, they were wrong. As the second half got underway we could see Geordies milling about

in the streets. The next forty minutes were spent deciding what
to do. We were up against it. We had to work out a plan to get
back to the station together or we were done – and with us
having one of the largest firms ever to visit the Geordies, we had
to make a show. We gathered downstairs until we were all
together, a move that did not go unnoticed either outside or
inside the ground. Geordies inside began to stream out to join
the firms waiting for us. It was pull up your pants and tie your
shoelaces time.

Grogan, Lewis, Pele, Willis, Fez, these much-respected lads
were at the front and we were not going to let them down. Two
hundred and fifty of us came out into the waiting Geordies. We
quickly did those in front of us and then turned right, where
more were charging forward. They were a rabble, not a tight firm
like us, and we ploughed into them. They scattered and we were
through and on our way. Things were looking good . . . but not
for long. We had gone through two streets when they came
again, what looked like thousands bouncing down the street
behind us. The police were doing their best to keep them back
but it was never going to last.

This was turning into one of the longest days. We got further
away from the ground, keeping tight, but some of the Geordies
had outflanked the police and were coming up fast behind us.
We turned, stood and waited for them. Their first wave was
spread out and they slowed as they realised we were going to
have it with them. We went toe-to-toe with the first wave, giving
out some serious slaps and kicks and bringing them to a stop.
The pressure, however, was relentless, with more of them
pressing from behind and bricks flying towards us.

Having brought the Geordies to a brief halt the lads began to
move on, but I was still at it and didn't realise it was time to go.
I was firing punches into one of their front men when another
Geordie smashed a brick into the side of my head and took me
out of the game. I went down, knocked out for a second or two.

Mick Brierley, from Wythenshawe, hauled me up, staying at my side even though he knew we had outstayed our welcome. The funny thing about it was that they didn't follow up on me, as they were intent on harassing the other lads. The first wave ignored me as they bounced past. That still left the hundreds following in their wake, but they too carried on by as we stood to the side. They hadn't seen anyone kicking us and must have thought I was one of their own, though they were head-to-toe in black and white while we wore no colours, as United's lads had discarded them a couple of years earlier. It must have been my lucky day.

We drifted through the streets and eventually managed to link up with the lads again. They'd had only a few more skirmishes and were only slightly dishevelled. Everyone was laughing and joking with relief; it had been one hell of a day. There was no sympathy for me, despite my aching head that clearly needed stitching. That's football violence for you. At least I had a story to tell, so it wasn't a bad day after all. A few cans of beer later and the pain was gone, along with any thought of having stitches.

The football violence in the Seventies taught us not to fear anything that came later, because you couldn't have got any madder than the Red Army days. No sensible person can explain how you could go down from a brick to the head, get up and go back for more. But I didn't want to miss anything, because it was the only excitement I had.

* * *

I WAS NOW one of the lads who was listened to. It was no longer a case of turning up at a ground in your thousands and laying waste; people like me were expected to lead the mob and get the tactics right. We had to be more canny. Nowhere was this more important than Leeds, a fixture where we had got it wrong for several years. I'd had murders up there in the War Wagon years and learned that you had to be on the ball when you crossed the Pennines or you were finished. This was the land of Neanderthals who didn't give a fuck. Leeds didn't distinguish between straight members and thugs, and that drove me mad. I cannot stand by and see ordinary fans beaten up, but Leeds were cavemen. It didn't help that the police were as thick as them and hadn't a clue. They left the ordinary supporter at the mercy of the mob, something which would never change over there.

I made it my aim to turn that around – and that's what happened when we went for a night match in the late Seventies. One hundred and fifty of us went on the service train, mostly the lads who had grown up into this life of violence over the past six or seven years, the likes of Coco, Phil Ritchie, Andy Owen, Pete Harrison, Mouse, Robbo and many more. I had told everyone that at the end of the game we'd turn right and walk up the road towards a social club. Just beyond a large car park was where we would all gather and then turn back without the police knowing. If we pulled it off we would be in a firm and would not have let anyone get behind us, as in the dark it's crucial to have everyone in your sights.

The game ended and we nervously made our way in little groups up the road, trying not to engage any Leeds, which would have destroyed the game plan. It seemed they were all up the other end of the road waiting, running round and making a noise but not doing much, as the police had cleared the area in front to give the fans on coaches a chance to run for it without too much mishap.

We waited for fifteen minutes in this car park with no Leeds hoolies about and, more importantly, no coppers. Then we headed back towards the ground, which was now clear of crowds. People were still about but they knew who we were and knew not to say anything. We also kept quiet; we knew there was a long way to go. I led the group up and then left on the opposite side of the road, taking us to the far side of the park and down the back roads through Holbeck and away from the main roads. The longer we marched, the more the nerves strained. We knew that if we were to encounter a large mob we would be stranded out in the open, and a running battle all the way to the station would probably be the end of us for the night, as we'd end up fighting more and more Leeds the further we went.

Luck was with us. All we encountered was the occasional pub with Leeds fans inside who knew not to venture out, as they could see this was a tight-knit firm. We didn't give them any grief, as we didn't want the police to come and spoil the surprise when we arrived through the back streets and entered the station from the opposite way they'd expect. We intended to attack without Leeds or the police even knowing we were there.

Just as we expected, Leeds were waiting in force at the station. We came round the corner undetected, charged up the ramp and ran them everywhere. Some tried to escape into the station and were trapped at the doors. We kicked them all over the forecourt and then blitzed through the station, which was now full of Leeds trying to escape over the barriers. They were piling up and we leathered into them. We chased them up and down platforms until there was nobody left to chase, every one of us now bouncing about, laughing and cheering. What a top night this had turned out to be – and it wasn't over.

We were all on the wrong platform, so the police moved us down the stairs and into the subway. To their credit, Leeds had come back; not, I suspect, to do us in but to save face – what was left of it. There must have been forty of them in the subway and I don't think they realised we were coming down or they wouldn't have bothered, as there was only going to be one result. A few were caught fleeing and were trampled on; the rest were chased back to the barriers, where they fought each other to get over. The police were on hand and we didn't push it, as we'd had a right result and to get anyone nicked would have spoilt it. Instead we retired to the train and back to Piccadilly. Fifty of us made our way to Kloisters nightclub for two hours to celebrate and do our victory dances. The tide at Leeds had turned. We now knew it was organisation, not numbers, that would win the day.

CHAPTER EIGHT

HOME AND AWAY

THE TRAVEL BUG bit me good and proper. Home games were great but away matches were where the real fun was to be had. I ran coaches now and then from my mid-teens onwards, mainly for lads from Wythenshawe at first. They were all mad drinkers. They would jump off the coach in the middle of whatever town it was and say, 'See you later, coach driver.' They didn't care how they got home; they were all bladdered on Party Sevens or bottles of cider and knew they could easily jump back on the special train anyway.

In December 1975 we became one of only three teams to ever take the Shoreham End at Sheffield United (the others were Leeds and Sheffield Wednesday). We took the biggest following ever seen there; huge groups were coming off trains from all over the country. Everyone made their way to the ground and little firms and big firms were going in their end. Eventually we took their end and forced them right to the top corner. They put up plenty of opposition – we had to fight like fuck to push them back there. But everyone in there was in for a fight and the sheer weight of numbers forced them back. United had the other end of the ground as well.

George Lyons: *The worst fight I was ever in was Sheff United away. We got there early. Their fans wore these tops that had a motif of like a house and a tree. They looked like mods. Sheff United scored in the last minute and lads went off their heads. The police came, a lot in plain clothes. It was murder. They had a good go but it kicked off everywhere. At the end they wouldn't come out, so we went round the ground from all sides, forced them out into the street and pasted them.*

To be honest, we never really saw ourselves just as fighters. We were more beer monsters than anything else; we would go for the pub. The young ones used us at times because when it kicked off they would use the confusion to hit the jewellery shops and then you wouldn't see them again for the day. We'd just get pissed and have a good scrap. Looking back now, you think it was a bit stupid, but it was part of growing up. You worked all week and at the weekend you looked forward to going out to the matches and having a drink with the lads. Apart from a bit of weed, the only drug we had was booze. It was good fun and they were good lads.

Burnley was another good away fixture in those days. They had a good team and a very loyal, parochial support. It was so near that I hitched it on the morning of the game. United fans were here, there and everywhere in their town. A pub opened its doors early and I got in. By the time normal opening hours came, it had gone off and the pub was wrecked. We had a proper set-to with some Burnley fans who regarded it as their pub; it had actually been opened for them, but we took advantage and got in before them. The pub ended up split half and half. By 11am the windows had gone in and that pub was not serving any more beers. There were a few cut heads on both sides before the police arrived.

We regarded the Longside at Turf Moor as their end but I didn't see any problem with United fans being in there. By the time I got in a lot of the fighting had already happened and that

A United fan dragged around the pitch at Burnley in 1973. Mass ejections from grounds were a feature of those years with the Red Army.

The infamous derby against Manchester City in April 1974 and United fans invade the pitch to halt the game. It was too late - we were already relegated.

Trouble at Leyton Orient away, the first game of our season in the Second Division, and a sign of things to come.

The Red Army at Ninian Park, Cardiff, in 1974, one of the most notorious games ever. The scenes of fighting after the match were indescribable.

Hitting the headlines: a picture of me as a long-haired teenage yobbo and a story about our legendary War Wagon.

TONY O'NEILL.
Met Sports Minister.

Fans' bid to avoid trouble hits a snag

YOUTH WORKER Andy Davies and the Crossacres Reds have found how to keep out of trouble going to Manchester United away games—by travelling on their own. But they have hit a snag.

By LAURIE BULLAS

The gang of United fans from Wythenshawe have been travelling together for 18 months in a mini bus. But Manchester education committee which owns the bus is worried and has banned the use of the bus for football trips.

Sport Minister Mr Denis Howell is so interested in the lads' trouble-free trips that he wants to talk to them when he comes to

organised trips have helped to keep them out of trouble.

Now they are hoping to buy their own van and plan to ask the education committee to tax and insure it for them—as it does for youth clubs.

FEARS

What the education committee fears is that it would be implented if some kind

"We were violent at the start because we had not been used to anything else. Once we got to know Andy we talked about it and reasoned it out . . . he has shown us the way we should go."

STEER CLEAR

Eric Hamnett, aged 20, of Broad Oak Road, who

Tottenham away and United fans bail out after making a bid to take a Spurs section. You always got a rumble at White Hart Lane.

Disorder at West Ham away in 1975, a game the whole East End had been waiting for since we had taken over Upton Park eight years earlier.

United fans on the North Sea ferry after the headline-hitting fight with West Ham in 1986. We were supposed to have been carried off on stretchers. Doesn't look like it, does it?

Howell's war on the thugs

-5 APR 1977

United face all-ticket away games after terror of Norwich

38 held after 'revenge' attacks

Savage fans leave a trail of terror

23 FEB 1976

ANGRY Manchester United fans went on the rampage after th...

By KEITH COLLING and ANDREW ...DLEY

...cut by ...hrough ...l and ...ses. ...tation ...caped ...sband ...dog. ...k to ...my ...him. ...ped.'

...e n ...s a ...the ...to

...d to ...h a

The ...ally ...em.' ...con- ...rols. ...use- ...t is ...king ...nds

...which ...st light

The trouble at Newcastle under Lyme started shortly after a coach carrying United supporters stopped at the Shakespeare Hotel.

'The fans came in for a drink and all of a sudden someone shouted "United, United," and the whole place just blew up,' said the manager, Mr Edwin Clunn.

"They were throwing tables, glasses, and chairs. They were fighting with everything they could lay their hands on.'

Stitches

"They just turned on my regulars and then they ran out. There was nothing I could do but bolt the doors behind them.'

One youth had 33 stitches in head wounds. Another was treated for cut wrists.

Mr David Smith, chairman of the Manchester United supporters' club, said: 'As far as I know it wasn't one of the official supporters' club coaches.

'None of our coaches would have stopped after a match like that.

'Our fans have been extremely well-behaved this season and shall certainly be looking against ...

... chief problem now is outside the grounds,' he said. But recent events have shown that to be wishful thinking.

Riot fans swing 15 ft rails at match

Sunday Express Reporter

DOZENS of Manchester United Soccer fans were hauled before special late-night courts in Nottingham last night after what police described as "horrific scenes" of violence at...

Headlines from our rampages. United's activities led directly to a government clampdown on soccer thuggery, the introduction of fences at grounds, segregation and ticketing restrictions.

Some of the lads in typical fashion of the time before a Wembley final in the mid-seventies.

Little Dessie *(left)* and Harry the Dog *(right)* on a pre-season foreign tour in the early Eighties. Harry once hit me with a fire axe - for a laugh!

Everton away in 1984 (see Chapter 13) and our 350-strong mob prowls through the streets of Croxteth on our way to Goodison.

If the football intelligence unit consider me the hooligan ringleader at United, why are four of them posing happily for a photo with my son - taken by me? Read more in my next book.

Little Dessie and myself, both now retired from past exploits. I'm currently banned from following United but the Old Bill are still on my case, for some reason. Oh well, they can't stop me writing!

was where I saw more skinhead birds. They seemed to be the only ones left. They got the usual treatment but I think they wanted to fight. They might have even got a dig or two.

Clubs like Burnley would put up a fight but the likes of Sunderland were in a different league again in the mid-Seventies. Roker Park was one of those places where you had to be on your mettle at all times. Loads of us went up on the special in the mid-Seventies and got off, I think, at Seaburn, from where we walked to the ground. The coppers in their wisdom brought us round past the Sunderland end, which resulted in us having it off and fighting with them. We charged through them and then charged round to our end, where we then hung around waiting for the payback. Sure enough, as time drew on they came round in little gangs and we were scuffling on and off for half an hour. In the end we had to go in the ground because it was coming on top.

We knew we would be in trouble afterwards. It is a long game when that happens – and we knew the coppers would be no use whatsoever. The end came soon enough and there was chaos outside in the street. We had to walk past their end again. There was no unified mob walking up that road; people came out, got caught in scuffles, saw what was coming and said, 'Hey, we're off here.' The idea was to get back to Seaburn without suffering a hiding, so everyone waited to nip through in the general disorder.

I got in a scuffle outside a house with a few of them and was helped out by some United fans on the road who backed me up and helped to chase them off. But we had all been split up and it was very difficult to hold any numbers together. We regrouped at Seaburn and it seemed that though there had been several clashes away from the stadium, things had not been as bad as they could have been. We boarded our train with a sense of relief, knowing we had been lucky.

Then one of the biggest blokes you will ever see in your life strode onto the platform at Seaburn station and challenged

119

everyone. He was a man mountain. He didn't have any colours, he was just a demented north-east nutter who paced ten yards forward, ten yards back, screaming abuse. I don't know if someone had shagged his daughter or run off with his missus, but he hated us. People returned abuse through the train windows, but though there were some very handy blokes on that train, not one got off. Even the coppers dared not move him, and when our trained pulled away he was still there, screaming blue murder. Anyone who went on that special will remember that monster.

* * *

IN THE WINTER of 1976, I decided to go to Turin for a cup game against the mighty Juventus. My plan was to hitch it with another lad off the estate called Palmer. I'd not been abroad under my own steam before and knew nothing about Italy, never mind Turin, but I got my one-year passport, looked at a map and said, right, Manchester to Dover to Calais, then looked at France and decided to go to Paris, then Lyon, then Grenoble. From there I would cross the Alps into Italy. Simple. I had no idea of distances, foreign languages, what the weather was going to be like, what the roads were like, nothing.

We gave ourselves a week to get there, leaving on a miserable Wednesday night for the game the following Wednesday. First, though, I went to see us beat Newcastle 7–2 in the League Cup at Old Trafford. The Geordies brought a few and I was outside with my bag trying to capture some of them with the other Manchester scallies. We chased two or three back into the ground, then set off for Italy in good spirits. I had £25 to my name.

It took us all night to get to Dover – we actually reached the port at 8am the next day. I had never even been on a boat before. We sat around waiting for the ferry when Palmer decided he'd had enough already and headed back. I always knew that as long as there was a British Embassy somewhere, I could find safety – I assumed they would look after their own. So off I went alone. I got to Calais, then started hitching to Paris. I made it, and spent Thursday night in a Paris railway station, where I dossed down, chatting to a few other people. I had a little holdall and wore my grey duffel coat.

I reached Grenoble on the Saturday. It was freezing – well, I was at the Alps, which loomed above the town. I started walking because I couldn't seem to get a lift. I didn't realise there was virtually no route and snow all over the mountains – it was early November by now. Eventually I was walking on the road to Italy, going up a mountain with my thumb stuck out. There was snow everywhere – and no traffic.

I came to a little village with a railway line running through it and into a tunnel under the mountains. By now I had realised I couldn't walk there but nor could I jump on a train – the only train there was a flatback shunter to take the trucks through the mountains. Things looked bleak. There seemed to be no cars, and even I wouldn't risk walking through the railway tunnel. I lay down on the snow and wondered what the hell I was doing there.

Salvation came in the form of a sudden convoy of Land Rovers with British plates. English, I thought, here we go. I stopped the first one to ask for a lift and they discovered were Italians who'd been to an auction in Wales to buy the cars and were driving them back. I tried to explain who I was and showed them my scarf but I don't think they had a clue. In the end they put me in the back of one of the Land Rovers and somehow explained that when they got to the other side of the mountains, they were staying the night because it would be getting dark.

We reached the Italian side of the Alps and they booked a the bed and breakfast. I was hoping to sleep on the floor of their room but instead they told me to stay in the car and disappeared inside for a nice hot meal. Oh well. I got my sleeping bag out of my rucksack, zipped myself in and tried to kip.

I woke up at 5am, shaking like I had never shook in my life. There was frost over the windows and heavy snow outside. I was blue with cold and my jaw chattered like maracas. I rubbed my shoulders and ribs to try to keep warm but it was no use. Then slowly the sun began to rise over the Alps into a clear blue sky. I could feel it heating me up, bringing me back to life. Fantastic.

At 7am the Italians came out, looking well fed and rested, the bastards, and dropped me off further along the way. From there I hitched into Turin. The problem was, it was only Sunday – and the match was not until Wednesday night. I did the usual thing, hanging about, chatting to people, scrounging meals and dossing at the railway station, but the time dragged.

Come Tuesday night I was expecting United to arrive. I was up and down the streets but couldn't see any. Unbeknown to me, wherever United fans went out drinking it was coming on top with Juventus fans, so they had all retreated to their hotels. I was starving, had spent all my money and was getting desperate. On Wednesday I spotted big Gibbo and was so pleased to see him. He took me to his hotel, fed me and put a bit of money in my pocket. I spent the rest of the day with United fans, who were now venturing out more as the numbers arrived. I personally saw no trouble before the game, but the threat of it hung in the air.

I'd had a lot of experiences by then, but inside the ground was like a different world. We were held in a corner seating section surrounded by soldiers. The Italians nearby were distinctly unfriendly and at the final whistle they started throwing things at our section. All these soldiers with rifles stood by doing nothing while we came under a heavy bombardment that showed no signs of abating. Our tormentors were to our right, separated from us by a metal gate, but for once no-one made a move towards them as we were wary of the soldiers.

Dave Smith, who ran the Manchester United Supporters' Club, had somehow got a megaphone and stood up to address the crowd. Dave was the voice of reason and was shouting, 'Don't react, sit down, relax, everyone keep calm, remember the good name of Manchester United.' No-one was kicking off as for once we were listening to him.

'Behave, lads.'

A half whisky bottle flew over from the Italian side. We watched in horrified fascination as it arced through the air, hit Dave's megaphone and sent him sprawling backwards. He disappeared from view behind the row of seats. There was a stunned silence – and then the top of the megaphone was seen to rise and we heard Dave's hysterical bellow:

'Fuck that! Get the bastards!'

And everyone was down the stairway and into them at the fence.

Dave, incidentally, was a fabulous man. He was respected for his integrity not just by the ordinary supporters but by the so-called hooligans as well. He knew us all by name, knew everyone that travelled and was a gentleman. The Supporters' Club in those days was very influential – eventually you had to be a member to buy a ticket for a game – but the club took it off him. As far as I'm concerned the bastards ripped him off, a diehard football fan who loved United.

Anyway, that incident set the tone. When we finally got out of the stadium, the streets were packed with dangerous-looking Italian youths. I decided I was going to the airport to get on a plane, regardless; the city would not be safe to hang around in. We headed to the coaches, which were parked alongside tram tracks. Suddenly there was no escort – the coppers just left us. By the time we had reached the first corner, thousands of Italians were closing in by the second. One started acting up in front of us, so one of the Gillham twins whacked him over the head with a flag. That started it. Next thing there were punches flying all over the place. We stuck together and got across the road. From there we looked back: there seemed to be a big black swarm moving ominously towards us, some of them pounding away on drums, others chanting in Italian. None of them seemed friendly.

We got around the coaches, dodging bricks and slabs. Some trams came past and caused a break in the brick-throwing. They were packed with Italians, so we came running from behind the coaches and showered them with every solid object we could get our hands on. One tram disintegrated under the onslaught and United fans were reaching in through the broken windows and snatching up flags as trophies.

Once the trams moved off they were back at us and we had to fight them off at the doors of the coaches. 'Defend the coaches,' people were shouting, trying to rally the troops. Eventually *carabinieri* turned up but the fans were still mad for getting us. Quite a few of our lot had cut faces and hands.

We were kept there on the coaches for another half hour, but at least we had survived. Then our coaches set off, and we had not made the end of the road when the onslaught of bricks began again. They thudded off the panelling like drumbeats. Our only escort was one cop van at the front which had its blue light flashing to helpfully tell everyone we were coming. We all lay on the floor as glass sprayed over us. Even the drivers' windows went in. People were screaming or yelling instructions:

'Keep driving.'

'Don't stop.'

'Get down.'

We got to this big roundabout and the drivers were going so fast they nearly turned the coaches over. One couldn't or wouldn't slow down and simply went straight over a mound in the centre of the roundabout and crashed down on the other side to rejoin the convoy. After that we were okay. We stopped a little further on and everyone got off to check for injuries. We were all happy to have got out alive.

We reached the airport and I decided I was getting on that plane, no matter what. Six others were without tickets and had to sneak on too. In those days you had a desk with one woman behind it, a pile of boarding cards and that was it. There was a plane going to London and we knew there were seats on it. One of the Gillhams grabbed the boarding cards and threw them up in the air. In the confusion the police assumed we were all on the plane and we charged through and got on. There were murders with the crew because after a head count they found they had 160 people instead of 153. Eventually they decided to let us stay because they couldn't work out who was who. The police tried to intervene but we were ducking and diving beneath the seats and in truth they wanted us out of there.

We landed in London and eventually got to Euston. I was shattered. I had no train ticket and no money – though I did have loads of Italian flags, which I had carried onto the plane. We got on the train and all fell asleep – and every one of us got caught jibbing. We had travelled all that way, only to get caught on the final leg home. I eventually got off at Gatley in the morning and walked all the way home but I was dead happy because I was back on the estate and none of my pals had been abroad. I felt like a retuning king and couldn't wait to tell them the stories.

Two doors down lived my neighbour, young Simmo, only a kid. I knocked on his door and his mum answered. 'Here you are, give him these,' I said, and handed her all my flags. I had decided there were no more collections to be had, no more buying programmes and no more nicking scarves. That side of the life had gone for me.

* * *

THOUGH THE ERA of truly huge away support was passing, there were still some games where we could get monstrous numbers into away grounds. At FA Cup matches, especially semi-finals, you were guaranteed a large ticket allocation, and in 1977 we played Leeds United in a semi at Hillsborough. It was so full I was locked out. It was unbelievable: we were playing Leeds in Yorkshire and we had three-quarters of the ground. One end was half United and half Leeds, and there was me stuck outside. What a bummer. There had already been fighting all the way to the ground and now it went off proper. We tried to kick in the gates but the coppers beat us back. In the end we had to disperse from around the ground but by then lots of Reds were up for it in their end. We could see them from outside making their move. George Lyons was the instigator.

George Lyons: *We were supposed to have one end of the ground and them the other but we actually had half of their end as well, with the police down the middle. At half-time, it kicked off a bit and I saw an old bloke with a walking stick, a Red, who looked a bit agitated.*

'Are you all right mate?' I asked.

'Yorkshire bastards,' he said.

'Here y'are, give us your stick.'

I borrowed his stick, put him against the wall, then hit this Yorkshire cunt right on the head with it and split it open. That was the signal. We steamed into them.

After the match we had to go into the town. Most of the United went the other way, to coaches, but we had come on the service train early in the morning. There was a big crew of them behind us and a lot of fighting. My mate got stabbed in the back. The police kept saying, 'Keep moving.' We got to the station and they came flying across the tracks to get at us but we booted them off – they couldn't get up onto the platform. There was a couple of thousand of them but there was 4–500 of us and that was enough.

We won 2–1 to set up a final against Liverpool, who that season were going for the Treble. I had planned to jib the all-night mail train to London but hundreds had had the same idea and the station was crawling with British Transport Police, so instead I cadged a lift with Kevin Bond from Wythenshawe. We got to a motorway service station and saw a coach of United fans from Blackpool, some of whom I knew, so we jumped on board.

The second we got on I thought, what am I doing on here? They were already off their heads; it was like walking into a packed pub at 10.30 on a Friday night when you are sober and everyone else is dancing on the tables. They were decked in scarves and coats and rosettes – I thought all that had died off, as the Manchester lads were wearing different gear by this time, but these were good-time nutters – and there was beer and piss everywhere, and people lying down in it. Those lads were pure alkies. Kevin and I were sober and could have done with a snooze to kill time on the journey but there was no way we were having a kip – no-one was allowed to nap unless they were unconscious.

When we pulled in at another service station, some of them staggered off and immediately started trouble with some Scousers. Plates were skimming around the cafeteria like frisbees. A couple of the Blackpool lads got smacked because they were too pissed to fight. I just watched and shook my head.

We got into London at 5.30am and the coach went straight to Wembley and parked up. A few others were already there. I desperately needed sleep by now and nodded off for an hour, only to be woken at 6.30 by shouting outside – someone had brought a football and found some Scousers who wanted a game. Of course, it didn't last long.

'Fight!'

'Scousers!'

Somebody tackled someone else a bit too enthusiastically, a scuffle started, the shout went up and next thing everyone was jumping off coaches and piling in. Some were that pissed and bleary-eyed they didn't even know they were at Wembley. I was straight off and running around chasing Scousers. The roar had gone up and you never ignored the roar.

Yet I didn't see any more trouble the whole of that day, and I was there all day waiting for it. I couldn't believe it. At least United won the game 2-1.

I wisely elected to get a different coach back. In those days they would put signs on the motorway saying, 'Coaches for Liverpool only', or whatever, directing different supporters to different service stations to prevent trouble. We saw the first Liverpool sign, so what do you do? You ignore it. We pulled up on the service station and saw six or seven Scouse coaches. Some of them had started on a few United fans who were in a car and were legging them across the petrol station. We pulled up, a coach full of lads, jumped straight off and chased these Scousers back to their coaches. There were scuffles on the car park as some of them fought back but we were right as rain as a firm and they couldn't touch us.

The Scousers drove off and we followed before the cops arrived, only for their coach to pull up on the slip road. I don't know what was going through the drivers' minds but our coach pulled up behind them and it was all off again. The Scousers ended up running back on their coach with us trying to smash the windows. They drove off and we got back on the coach shouting, 'Follow that coach, we'll have them at the next stop.' It was mad.

Despite winning the FA Cup, Tommy Docherty got the boot that July. A lot of United fans were gutted. I met him a few years later at an airport and he was a pleasant bloke. He was right for us; he got his players to attack and had the feel for what we wanted. It didn't matter with Tommy's team if you lost a game; even when we were relegated, you could feel what he was all about. The biggest disgrace was sacking him after the final, especially when you had Martin Edwards there, who has been shagging prostitutes all his life. And Doc had just won the Cup final playing football that we loved, with wingers. Dave Sexton replaced him. He was a knobhead who had no rapport with the fans. I don't think he ever spoke to any of the fans.

The club had other troubles. In April 1977, United had wrecked Norwich. This was the infamous game where a fan was filmed falling through the corrugated iron roof at Carrow Road and crashing onto the terraces below. Thirty-eight people were injured and the Barclay Road Stand was trashed. It provoked the most furious backlash yet from my mate Denis Howell and the Labour Government. Howell called in League secretary Alan Hardaker and the chairman and secretary of the FA for urgent talks. It was decreed that United fans would only be allowed to buy seating tickets at away games, and even that was at the discretion of the home club. Seating areas were relatively small in those days, so in effect they were banning United fans from travelling. United were also told to drop the recognition of many of the supporters' club branches outside the city, to stop hooligans descending from all over the country.

Yet very few of our terrace rivals had the confidence to take us on at home. Only once did I see Cockneys travel up in large numbers in the mid-Seventies and that was by coach with police escorts. The mob was Spurs and they had a mighty impressive firm, but even they knew that they would be escorted and kept in. There was no getting the train to Piccadilly and taking the walk to Old Trafford and back for them.

The first sign that Chelsea were feeling their way came in September 1977 at Old Trafford. We had not played them for three years because, despite their famous and massively overrated team of the early Seventies, they had fallen into Division Two for a couple of seasons. The mighty Chelsea, as they see themselves, had already appeared in the first televised post-match ruck, fighting on the pitch at Derby, had the highest arrest rate in London and had caused havoc in Division Two. That sent out the message that we were being challenged.

We'd always gone down there – for Bobby Charlton's final game before retirement we had overrun Stamford Bridge, and on another occasion thousands had been locked out of the away end and so had gone onto the famous Shed and not been removed. That was the difference between United and Chelsea: we didn't worry about there being no segregation and the prospect that we might get filled in. Whatever happened, happened. It didn't bother us.

Yet here's a fact for all you hooligan historians out there: Chelsea never came to Old Trafford as a mob on a train. Never. They were frightened to put themselves on offer in Manchester because if they got done, there was the Chelsea name gone. They tended to declare fuck all. Instead they'd come up in coaches and cars, in small groups, and meet at some out-of-the-way place. They never came into Manchester and took it to us in the city centre. Not like the Scousers in the early Seventies, when the police were wank, and in the Eighties to their credit, and even once or twice in the Nineties when they at least came on the train and got off in a firm. The Cockneys have never done that.

Anyway, the day was set, and as usual the city centre was full. Wherever you went, groups were looking for the mob of Chelsea. Well, they didn't show, at least not as an organised, aggressive firm. Just the opposite.

This was what one of the national newspapers had to say:

Blue Line Saves The Fans
It took 1,200 Chelsea fans 15 minutes to shuffle 400 yards to safety after their team had beaten Manchester

United 1–0 at Old Trafford on Saturday. And they only made it because a thin blue line of 200 police officers kept at bay a howling 3,000 strong mob of fanatics who regard themselves as United's 'Red Army'.

Like a guerrilla army, the United hooligans melted away when squads of police cleared the quarter-mile route from the football ground to Warwick Road station.

But they had hid in side streets, down back entries, behind parked cars and at nearby blocks of flats ready to ambush Chelsea supporters on their way back to the trains.

The police, under Chief Supt James Clayton, had mounted a containment plan like a military operation. They detained the Chelsea fans inside the ground for 30 minutes after the final whistle.

Then, with mounted policemen and dog handlers acting as outriders, the heavily guarded convoy moved off along the previously cleared route.

Some of their boys did come to Old Trafford that day, however, and what an embarrassment for them. You've heard of White Van Man, well that was Chelsea: forty of them in the back of three white Transit vans – pure class for well-groomed cockneys with loads of money but no bottle. They got in the ground safely, were locked in for half an hour after the game and then slunk back to their vans. This was the mighty Chelsea, who'd been giving it the big one in London at the height of football hooliganism. But they now knew it was safe to visit Old Trafford, as the police would keep you in and look after you. There was no turning up and 'whatever happens, happens' for them.

The three vans stopped at the Royal Crown Hotel near Manchester Airport on their way home. It was a pub isolated next to a slip road to the motorway. The only people in there were couples – it was a nice, quiet watering hole – but some of the locals got to hear about these Chelsea making a noise in the bar. Some of them, led by Mick Brierley's brother Terry, a hard nut on our estate, led a band of twenty who had nothing to do with football but fancied having it with some Cockneys. I don't think between them they had ever seen a Cockney or visited London, but they fancied a punch-up.

Into the pub they marched and Terry Brierley waded into the first Cockney with his iron bar. Then the pub just went up, with the Chelsea fighting back. They opened their vans, brought bats back into the pub and did some damage. One man out with his missus was lucky to survive and ended up with a few operations to relieve the pressure on his brain. The mighty Chelsea were reduced to brawling in a car park then scrambling in their vans while trying to get back up the motorway slip road. Not for long though as the police rounded them up and nicked them.

This was the *Daily Mirror* the following Monday:

Staff and customers fled in terror as 100 rampaging thugs laid into each other with bottles, glasses and pieces of furniture. Damage totalled more than £1,000. Fifty people were taken to hospital and one Manchester man suffered a fractured skull. The vicious brawl erupted late on Saturday night as Chelsea fans celebrated their 1–0 win over United. 'They had been lively all evening,' said pub landlord Alan Panter. 'Suddenly I heard a shout of, "Come on you bastards," and all hell broke loose.' Thirteen windows, twelve chairs and six stools were smashed as fighting spilled out into the car park. Police held forty-nine fans overnight.

Terry Brierley was jailed for five years and a few cockneys were sent down, which was not to their liking as Strangeways was no picnic back then. Chelsea took a few more years before they came back to Manchester with any confidence.

The scene was set for the return at their place the following February. The problem was, they refused to sell us any tickets. Well, we didn't care. We were going to London to take them on. We didn't need tickets, we were coming. The odds were that we'd get weighed in, but so what? We were United.

Who else would have done what we did?

We planned to meet at Piccadilly Station. Someone promised they would have coaches there, but most wanted to go on the train, and so 200 of us boarded the service, no fanny merchants and no coppers. We were straight on without tickets. As far as the authorities were concerned, we didn't exist, so why should we buy tickets? The hectors got nothing and the ticket inspectors were invisible. It was mob rule.

We arrived at Euston to find only a few Cockney Reds, for once, and made our way straight to the tube. A couple of coppers stood on the train with us but said nothing. I don't think they could figure us out. We got off at Fulham Broadway, which was full of police and lined with horses on both sides of the pavement. We had no plan because we hadn't expected to get this far. Chelsea were all there, hanging out of the pubs. On the left was a load of shops. We knew Chelsea liked to loiter in those shops and then slip out and try to mingle with you, but today the coppers held them back. The odd smart-arse who did creep swiftly got a dig.

They escorted us to the entrance, where we found a few straight United fans. Incredibly they let us pay in; they must have figured they'd rather have us in the ground than running around the streets. But where were they going to put us? Half the terrace was occupied by Chelsea fans and the other half was empty. We got in and saw there were no police up the walkway to the terracing, which was a bit of a mistake on their part. We stood at the back to the left hand side and waited for everyone to get in. I looked around and saw the likes of Fez and Jimmy Miller from Salford. There was going to be no messing with these lads. Chelsea had some of their lads in there too but for a while nothing was said. Eventually a scuffle broke out, enough to get us all together. The coppers came in and the scuffle seemed to sort itself out.

We were now isolated, in a tense situation. The cops surrounded us so nothing was going to happen during the match but all Chelsea eyes were on us. We knew what was coming. The game was little reprieve; it served only to increase the tension as the minutes ticked by.

The end finally arrived and they kept us in to let the home fans disperse. When they finally brought us down to the gate, the road outside was still chocker with Chelsea, and they were going nowhere. They tried to surge towards us and I saw Babs, their infamous one-armed leader, flying about outside the gate. He got a bit too carried away and the police carted him off.

They finally brought us out and kept us on the road, with Chelsea trying to get at us and infiltrate from both pavements. Some of us were getting smacked, some of them were getting smacked. It must have taken half an hour to get down the street to the tube station. They tried to clear the front of our path but Chelsea were everywhere. Eventually the police forced their way through and put us on a platform on our own. A straight-member train came in and we filled two carriages. The doors shut and suddenly there were no police and no Chelsea. A communal sigh of relief was breathed. We reckoned we were out of the fire.

We had reckoned, however, without Kensington High Street. While the bulk of Chelsea's barmies had been trying to get at us in the street, the hardcore of their boys had gone on ahead to prepare the mother of all ambushes. As our train slowed into

Kensington, we saw that the platform was absolutely full of them – and no police. This was it; they'd pulled the perfect move and they were going to have us. The train stopped. We looked at each other and then back out at them. You could see the evil glee on their faces. This was their chance to claim the title of Britain's number one hooligan mob and they were going to take it with both hands.

The doors opened.

Bang, they were in at us. I knew that if they got a foothold in our carriage we'd be slaughtered, so I held onto the pole in the middle and swung both feet at a big bastard trying to get through the door first. Twice he tried to lead them in and twice I booted him off. With everyone else standing firm, we managed to knock them back off the train, and then the doors shut. The train remained stationary, however. Chelsea tried to smash the windows and prise open the doors, but the brief respite gave us time to get over the initial shock of their ambush. We had held them off.

As the windows went in, I saw a straight member sitting with his missus, holding a drinks bottle. I grabbed it off him and sent it flying through the shattered window. Then a seat went through at them. Still the train refused to move and we knew the doors would open again. We braced ourselves and prepared to go for it. We were all lads. This was what we were there for. We could see Chelsea wondering what we were going to do.

Suddenly the doors opened and I saw Coco go through one to my left and into them. I flew out, grabbing a red fire bucket they had slung at us. Andy Owens was beside me and now everyone was piling off.

'Off, get off! Come on, everyone, get into them!'

Chelsea backed away, unsure – and we blasted into them. For probably thirty seconds it was an orgy of pure, brutal, chaotic scrapping. Blokes were getting punched, butted, kneed, slung over, trampled and wellied. The din inside the station was

135

incredible as both sides lashed out with buckets and brushes that must have come from a railman's hut. It was a double platform with plenty of space and we drove a wedge between their forces. Some of them began to run up the stairs. Others were trapped at the far end of the platform and jumped onto the tracks to escape.

Somehow we cleared the platform. We were jubilant, but we knew the majority who had run up the stairs would be regrouping in the concourse and we couldn't let them counter-attack. So we went straight up after them, over the barriers and out into the street – and nobody was there. They had fled. We charged down the street to look for them, until someone spotted a diversion: a clothes shop with racks of leathers outside. The more enterprising lads took time out to help themselves to clobber. Further up the street we could hear sirens and see flashing lights and we knew our fun was over. We were delirious. We had gone there against all the odds, and we had blitzed them.

On the first day of the following season, Chelsea used exactly the same tactic against Everton, ambushing them at Kensington High Street and taking them apart. Perhaps by then they had perfected the technique, but it hadn't worked against us.

* * *

AS I HAVE already said, Highbury was always a favourite venue of ours, particularly for the Cockney Reds. In the Seventies you always found United fans behind the goal in the North Bank, a lot of sturdy lads but not the major mob because it wasn't as organised then; it was faces from here and there, a few Cockneys, and those that loved a drink. By the late Seventies we had become a proper fighting firm and now you had all the main Cockneys and Mancs together. On this particular day we were in a mob of 300 and all got on the North Bank, led by Black Sam.

We went over the turnstiles as usual with a simple plan: mob up and attack.

Our group grew as more and more arrived. Arsenal saw us but didn't attack straight away, foolishly letting us all come in and up the steps. Once everyone was there, the charge was on. Up the steps we went, led by Sam and a few others. After a few digs, the Arsenal at the top backed off and we got on the terracing. Now the rest of them piled over as everyone was trying to get stuck in. Eventually we were all there but the North Bank was swaying towards us and coming behind us. We were forced to the bottom as coppers tried to move in. As the surge came at us we were going down the stairway on the terracing. I was lashing out at everyone and getting it back on the back of the head. The priority, as ever, was not to go on the floor. We fought our way to the front, with them forcing us down. In the end we got out of there. Some dived over the wall, some fucked off into the crowd. We all knew when we went in that it would be on top but we had gone for it.

I think this was a big difference between us and some of the newer firms, particularly cockneys, who came up in the early Eighties. They all seemed to be concerned with not getting done. They wanted to protect their precious reputations at all costs and would not risk humiliation, so they only fought on their own terms. To me humiliation did not exist. If we got done, we got done. If the plan went wrong – if we got chased through the streets of Leeds like dogs after some moody night match – then so what? It has happened to us all and there might be anger at the time but we were there for the fight. I wasn't interested in hooligan league tables. Whatever happens, happens, was my motto.

There is no such thing as the hardest mob but I will say this: while we had clashes with all the big London clubs, anyone with brains will tell you that Tottenham was the most violent. This was because of the situation of the ground, the fact that the away end is right next to the street, and because of that long, moody walk back to Seven Sisters tube station.

Tottenham came to Old Trafford firmed-up on coaches towards the end of the Seventies and in our eyes had thrown down the gauntlet. We had no hesitation in picking it up, and in the 1978–9 hundreds of us met around Euston, all boys, no scarves, and headed off to north London. That day saw a massive explosion of violence down Seven Sisters. We all kept together and we were excellent that day. It doesn't matter who you are, when you have a mob that big you are going to win the first battle. And that wasn't even one of our biggest mobs.

CHAPTER NINE

THE MEN FROM
THE MIDLANDS

THE MIDLANDS HAS always been trouble. Matches there drew in our huge fanbase from the four corners of the nation, and the home mobs always geared up to meet us. Games against United were like cup finals for them, and though they were almost always overpowered they gave some good accounts of themselves. Be it Aston Villa, Birmingham City, Derby County, Leicester, Nottingham Forest, Stoke or West Brom, we knew we'd be in for an all-action day whenever we came visiting.

Typical was a day at Wolves in the cup in the mid-Seventies. At Old Trafford all they'd had was a corner of the Scoreboard End, a few fans but no mob. Off we went to their place for an evening return knowing it would be a different story at Molyneaux. We'd had good fights with Wolves in their town on a couple of occasions and sure enough it was pandemonium outside the ground. Gates were getting booted in, one of many times that happened, and we filled the whole end. A lot more people were in that ground than should have been and the atmosphere was brilliant. We were losing 2–0 and everyone was into it because we got back to 2–2 and then went 3–2 ahead. Our end was rocking, while they were going mad.

We came out to scrapping in every nearby street. It wasn't organised: the ground emptied and as the crowd all made their way to the town centre, fights spontaneously erupted everywhere. I had one vicious fight in a car park, then reached the town centre only to be charged at by a much bigger gang of Wolves. We had to whip round the corner with them on our heels. More Wolves and United arrived and now the whole town centre seemed to be consumed by a series of sporadic running battles; there was no one mass brawl, it seemed to be different gangs against each other.

Leicester City could be another moody trip. They're a proud bunch who think they are the heart of England, but they are another mob who never tried anything at Old Trafford. We went there for the last away game of the season in April 1976. Our fans were all down one side and squeezed into a section behind the goal. This would have an effect on the day's events, as to get in we effectively had to queue up outside their end.

The fighting started an hour before kick-off, with Leicester trying to get round to their own end but being stopped and chased around the back streets by the United hordes. I was with a firm of lads who were on average about seventeen: Phil, Harvey, Ritchie and Bondy, who happened to be a Blue. These lads were also grafters who would have keen eyes to make a bob or two when the opportunity arose. We had been at it on and off for half an hour when the real fighting started on the corner. United made a push for Leicester and were forcing their way round to the home end. We were all battling, with people going down on both sides. The police were in the thick of it but United's weight of numbers won the day. All the police could do was make a barrier between us and let us in the ground.

The game was like a long tea-break, with both sides champing at the bit to renew hostilities. Straight after the whistle, we were trying to get at each other, with the police again in between. All hell broke loose, with bricks flying. It was time to move into the side streets and that's when true chaos descended, as the police were nowhere. United charged at Leicester non-stop, right into the town, turning over cars and smashing windows all the way. Leicester had been done – or so I thought.

The town centre flooded with police vans and sirens but a few of us were still looking for a fight. We soon came across a bunch of Leicester and, with the euphoria of the day's action, we got carried away with ourselves and chased them – right into a trap. As we legged after this group, more of them piled into us from a side street. They hit us hard and many of us were lucky not to go down straight away, but the old adrenalin kept us up.

We had to get on our toes and now it was our turn to be split up and hunted down. Three or four of us were being hotly pursued and, as usual, there was one who was not going to make it, as he was too fat and unfit. Quick as a flash a shop door was kicked open and we all dived in, screaming to be saved from the mob behind us. The shop was wrecked within two seconds, not by the mob but by us as we dived over counters, over racks, over anything that got in our way. No way were we going to be caught. The bloke who owned the shop went bananas as we threw whatever we could grab towards anyone who came through the door. Fortunately it was soon over; none of the Leicester wanted to be first in, and also they were being watched by a large crowd of fascinated shoppers. So they moved off.

We left through the front door without having to open it, as there was no glass left, and gave a cheery wave and a thank you to the owner, who looked like his world had fallen in. I'm afraid that didn't matter to us; our priority was avoiding bumping into more trouble. I knew I'd have plenty more trips to Leicester to enjoy and there was no point pushing it – we'd used up all our luck for that day.

* * *

PLACES LIKE DERBY, Coventry and Villa were beanos for us. Derby got to a point where you would turn on the news the week before we played them and see the residents around the ground boarding up their property and signs saying, 'Please do not smash my windows.' Coventry was similar. I can't remember much trouble there because we always took so many that we were untouchable. We came out after one game in the Seventies, got to the parkland at the bottom of the road and a big fight erupted. As we ran across the park in the dark I couldn't tell who was who, and I'm sure it was United fans fighting each other.

I had been to Aston Villa in the War Wagon and collapsed in a drunken stupor (see Chapter Three). The following year I went on the train, sober and with the main lads. We were skirmishing almost straight away in Birmingham city centre and it continued at the ground, coming to a head when we tried to enter the Holte End. Villa piled round the corner and stood with us trading punches in the street until the police forced us back down towards our end. We split into smaller groups to try to get back up towards Villa, hoping to blag past the police. Some of us managed it but really we were only treading water, as we knew we could only go so far; Villa were everywhere, waiting.

I was in one of the groups and hung around, waiting for it to go. It wasn't long before Villa sussed us and were in and around us, trying to force us back. It was time to see what they were made of. We put up the shout and stood and traded punches with them. The good thing for me was that I was with big Fred Henshawe from Stretford and the O'Bane brothers from Sale, and we held our own until the police arrived again. These lads on many occasions were some of the gamest amongst us, and respect between us all from incidents like this made us into a fighting firm. We learned to hold it together against long odds when most would have backed off.

One thing about Villa was that no matter how hard you tried, you could never get a mob into the Holte End. We always wanted to take it and did get in there on occasions, but it near-impossible to get mobbed up and mount a charge. The only time we had decent numbers in there was when some of the Brummie Reds infiltrated, and they were rarely in for long. They were game and they'd fight for their lives but they knew more than anyone it wasn't going to work out. We'd catch up with them after the game and they'd explain that they were happy to go in and risk a kicking because they looked on it as personal between them and Villa. Mad they were, one and all.

My first trip to Birmingham City was in the early Seventies when thousands flocked to St Andrews and the special trains were packed. St Andrews has always been a tough place to visit; George Lyons once had an axe pulled on him by a half-caste lad down in the toilets. George did the decent thing and grassed him up to a copper! For this visit everyone I knew seemed to be there and what a day it was as we flooded through the city centre. We reached the ground in such numbers that there were few incidents, even though the police just let you go without escort. Thousands of United fans wandered around outside the ground and it was obvious the Red Army was slowly oozing towards enemy territory, unopposed.

It was about half one when the group I was with went through the turnstiles. We were down the side of the ground, which was their end, and already Reds were in large groups in the middle and to our right, some with scarves but loads there without. Familiar faces caught the eye, exchanging knowing looks and winks, letting you know they were sound and acknowledging that your firm was in and safe. You knew if you saw certain faces that others would be nearby, so seeing Big Dave from London let you know that Pancho, Bob, Sam and the rest of their lads were there even if you couldn't immediately see them. I saw Yowdy and Little Des, so Salford were there, saw Mouse, that meant Collyhurst were in, Harry the Dog was there, the list went on.

We all waited for the sign and it came at 2pm. It's wonderful to experience and never loses its appeal to me: like the noise of buffalo stampeding and then an almighty thud as two groups come together. That noise and that buzz I've heard loads of times and it never changes. United charged along the back of the stand into the Brummies, who held the top stairway entrance in the middle of the terracing. I didn't know until later that there was also a big scrap going on at the bottom of the stairs, and only the police breaking it up delayed the inevitable. The United group ran up their stairway and then ran across at Birmingham, joined by others on the way. We were two-thirds of the way down and tried to get to the action but it was now going off everywhere. This was a riot and no mistake, and everyone was loving it.

I had my legs taken from me twice and had to scramble up before I was trampled on. We were like two fields of corn swaying in the wind back and forth. Anyone who fell was kicked and stamped with steel-toed boots, the official thug wear of the time. Everything was being used – bricks, bottles, sticks, *nunchakus* – and casualties fell on both sides. Cops were going down as well, smashed aside as two cities went to war.

It ended in a stalemate. United could not remove them from their half and Birmingham couldn't dislodge us, so the police split the stand down the middle. Of course nobody watched the game; we spent ninety minutes hurling insults and debris back and forth. I don't know what the score was, it didn't matter – I don't think it ever really mattered back then, as you built yourself up all week for the aggro, not the football. Mad, I know, but that's how it was, good old working-class people doing what they have always done to each other.

Things were different the next time we played at Birmingham on a Saturday. Segregation was now in force though there was still no change with the police, who were even slower to see and react to the day's events. We came off the service train and out of New Street Station in time for pub opening, 250-handed. You could feel this was different – the vibe was altogether more threatening. Roaming round for the first ten minutes, we kept alert, as we found out there had been one or two little skirmishes with lads who had arrived earlier from different parts of the country.

We eventually settled down in a boozer, only for the police to arrive at 2.30 and force us towards the ground. The march went without incident and we were corralled outside the away end. We decided to whip round the corner and try to pay in the home section. Amid the crowds outside, about 150 of us off the service train managed to get away and quickly paid through. We kept our mouths shut. The funny thing was, I knew, and so did the others, that we were going to get twatted all over once we were discovered. However, the blood was pumping and the fear was overtaken by a shared high from knowing we were together. This was what it was all about, testing yourselves.

We got in and up the stairs and found ourselves at the back of a section near the corner flag. We could see a large empty section to our right, separating both sets of fans. I looked over into our section and knew that they were waiting for the action, as they were looking at the Brummies and knew it was coming.

It came all right. We were at the top when we unleashed the war cry. The look of shock on the Brummies in our corner section was priceless as we started dishing it out to anybody who stood their ground. Things went well for the first minute as we scattered them. I could hear this deafening noise from all corners of the ground, as though everybody had been waiting and waiting, then all let out a huge roar of relief at once. Only there was no relief for us, as our show of force had brought it on top in fine style. We were attacked by the hordes down the side.

Boots and fists thudded into faces and ribs, and while they were trying to batter us senseless, we were fighting to survive.

We quickly realised it was offmans but were faced with trying to scale a large wire fence. We finally made an undignified exit over barriers and down to the front, where some of the lads scrambled over. I was trapped halfway with Derek Whittaker and Andy Owen. We knew we had to stay on our feet even as we were getting smacked from all sides. Only with luck did we get out of there. Owen eventually climbed the fence and Whittaker and I scrambled over and onto the dirt track, with a few boots helping us on our way.

Once back in United's section, everyone was talking over each other about how great it had been, even though it was a suicide mission. For the ninety minutes of the game we either discussed what had happened or looked forward to the inevitable rematch outside at the end.

We were out early and saw various small groups forming outside our end, sussing each other out and egging each other on. It was only a matter of time before it went off and in situations like this you say to yourselves, don't wait, there's no point – you kick it off before the opposition get it together and the police box you in. Fifty of our main firm grouped up. We all knew what to do; there was no screaming or shouting, we went straight into the nearest crowd of Brummies and right through them. Then we were onto the next ones, who didn't stay for a fight.

Suddenly all these little groups were running, being chased by us back around the corner. We didn't pursue them as we didn't want to push our luck and there were now a few police about, with the odd horse galloping around. As soon as we had finished congratulating ourselves on fucking them off, back they came, not all the way but they certainly showed with a firm: there were 4–500 running towards us, with more pouring out from the ground. We made a little stand but not for long; their

146

numbers were too great. As we ran back we saw coppers at the United end swinging their truncheons to keep the rest of the Reds inside the ground. I had to swerve one or two swipes and found myself on an overgrown patch of derelict land opposite – on my own. Well, not exactly on my own: I was surrounded by Birmingham bootboys throwing bricks at the away end.

The scene descended into carnage, with coppers on horseback charging into the Brummies, who had now massed into their thousands. The United fans inside were going berserk trying to get out, while the Brummies in the street ran amok. My problem was two-fold: I was in danger of getting smashed if the police got me, or obliterated if I was sussed as a Red. Yet I had to stay near too, as it wouldn't be long before the rest of the lads forced their way out.

I did the sensible thing and ducked down among the grass and weeds. Nobody noticed, though I was still in danger from a brick or one of those big fucking stallions galloping by. Once or twice I nearly came a cropper as the cavalry charged past. United eventually forced their way out. I rose from the grass like a member of the SAS, and before joining the Reds, I punched some startled Brummie who was in the midst of throwing a brick. If he's still alive today I guarantee he will never have had a bigger shock than me appearing from the weeds and smacking him in the mouth.

The police forced both sets of supporters in different directions but the two sides came together again at every junction or patch of ground to scrap it out. We clashed all the way back to New Street. Reaching the station was a relief for all, as it had been touch and go whether we could hold them back on the way. Everyone agreed it had been a cracking day, with everyone getting stuck in and the only bad injuries being cut heads from flying bricks and the odd bloody nose or mashed lip.

It wasn't unusual back then to see people clutching their heads with large open wounds and blood pouring down over them. On a few occasions I fell victim to a house brick or bottle and we would always be told by the local police to 'Fuck off and get stitched when you get back to Manchester.' Many a time you would also hear the immortal words, 'You wanted to fight, so fuck off.' At least it spared many a Red from getting nicked.

* * *

ANOTHER PLACE I enjoyed going was Stoke. It's only an hour's drive from south Manchester and was always a proper day out for the lads, as we would always have a fight and sometimes a riot outside, with both sides going for it. In the early years you would always get United fans in their end and always the same faces – Jeff Lewis, Pancho, Big Dave from Warrington – would end up behind the goal. Later, as segregation and all-ticket matches were introduced, things changed and United were sometimes on the receiving end.

One of those times was a night match in 1977. After the game we were going under a railway bridge when Stoke unexpectedly piled into us from behind. Anyone worth their salt knows it's difficult to hold it when you can't make out who, where and how many there are. We were lucky to keep it together until we rounded the corner and then managed to turn and back them off, but they had done damage and a few of us had fat lips once again.

That was nothing compared to the time we were outside the United end, hanging around waiting for the move towards their end. A few of us had been having little scuffles up and down the main street for half an hour and it was only a matter of time before everything blew. Our sporadic action was drawing crowds who were getting interested. Looking back, the scene was typical Red Army aggro, lads milling about with red and white scarves around their wrists, scarves wrapped around their foreheads and dangling from their waists. There were skinheads all in

148

denim, with six-inch turn-ups on their jeans to show off their cherry red Docs, some with butchers' coats on with writing all over, others with long hair, a proper clash of styles. It was the crossroads of football fashion, with some ready to move on, some clinging to being skins and some who still loved the butcher's coat. Some of the clothes were cringeworthy but we were united by a common aim: to have a go at getting down the opposite end and getting in.

The shout duly went up and soon became a roar. We started to walk, then trot, then run down a street level with the main stand. This was war – that's how we saw it, and many a time this scene was played out up and down the country. Those people in the street parted smartly – they knew to get out of the way, and there was nothing stopping this lot. We reached the Stoke end and went straight into them. They fought back as they always did but we backed them round the corner by weight of numbers. Everyone was lashing out in the melee and, being at the front as usual, I was crushed between United and Stoke and took a few cracks from both sides. It didn't matter as the adrenalin took over and I didn't feel a thing.

Stoke gamely hung on as more and more United swarmed round the corner. Then the cavalry arrived: several cops on horseback swinging their batons onto our heads backed up by dog handlers. You can't win in that situation and reluctantly we were forced back, happy we had made our mark. During the confusion, some United got into the Stoke end, helped by their colours as both teams were red and white. I couldn't make their end but jumped the turnstiles further down, as did scores of others.

Inside we could see things warming up for those in the Stoke end. United gathered in a top corner and fights broke out, but there were not enough to hold their ground. They were forced down behind the goal, where they made another stand. This had happened to me on a previous visit and my pals and I had ended up having to leap over the fence and scramble into the paddock before they dragged us down.

On this occasion we had to watch, frustrated, as fists flew for most of the first half. This was no good for most of us, as we wanted to get back into the aggro. That's what we were there for. The second half we spent outside, seeing if anything was going on or if we could start something, but it wasn't until twenty minutes before the end that others joined us. I made my intentions plain.

'Come on, as soon as we've got a few more we're going round their end. Let's give it these Stoke bastards.'

We waited for a few extra to join us, then with ten minutes of the game still to play we were off. We strolled down this time, no shouting, making sure we got there without drawing attention. We rounded the corner and were into a few Stoke outside, chasing them back in through the open gates. I followed them in, swinging my boot at anyone near me. But when I looked back over my shoulder, I couldn't understand why only a few had followed me in.

'Come on, fucking hell, what are you doing? Let's get into them.'

I soon knew why they were reluctant. The steps up to the terraces in front of me filled with Stoke hooligans – and then they charged. To stand would have been suicide – there were hundreds of them and anyway you can't fight uphill – and the others behind me were already disappearing, so I turned and ran, with the nearest Stoke lads right on my case. I needed to get to the gates before them and luckily I made it. There was no stopping as the mob continued to pour out behind me and a big fat cunt in particular was right on my case. We've all been there before, thinking why me, and I was doing some nice dance steps to ensure his boots weren't connecting.

Luckily the dreaded hand didn't grab my collar. Things were looking okay; another couple of yards and I'd be away, and so would the others. We were not strong enough nor the mob big enough to take this charge on – or so I thought.

What I hadn't banked on was that our lot would choose this moment to attack the Stoke coming behind me. I was the meat in the sandwich. As both sides came together in a blur of knuckles and boots, I bore the brunt from both sides. I think the fat twat chasing me got his kicks in, because I had some spectacular bruises in my back later. After bobbing around like a cork in a storm, I managed to fight my way into a space and was relieved to see the police break it up.

CHAPTER TEN

MAXIMUM SECURITY

BY THE LATE Seventies, our rivalry with the Scousers had developed into what can only be described as hatred, partly I suppose because Liverpool were doing so well on the pitch and we weren't. Whenever we had a chance to put one over on them, it lent special excitement to a fixture. In 1979 we played them in the FA Cup semi-final at Maine Road. I honestly can't remember much about the game, though I know they brought a firm and there was a lot of trouble. The old memory is not what it was. The result was a 2–2 and so it was over to Goodison on a Wednesday night for the replay.

We went on the service train with a big firm of lads – all the faces were there. No-one could touch us before the game and hence there was not much fighting. We won 1–0, putting us into the final (against Arsenal) and knew they would be out for our blood afterwards. We came out into a compound where they held you before releasing you into the streets. Fez and a few others said, 'We should wait here.' I was ready to go straight out and take them on but it was pitch black and there was some uncertainty, so we ended up standing and waiting in this compound – hundreds of us from the service train. We could hear the Scousers outside.

We gave it a couple of minutes and then came out behind them. They had gone down Stanley Park on the way to Scotty

Road. When we got down there they were in the side streets and although we filled the road, it was dark and proper moody. We knew this was where it would kick off. The police were not in control and we spread onto both sides of the pavement in preparation for the onslaught.

They couldn't stop us pressing forward down the dip to Scotty Road. The Scousers were at the bottom of this dip and it looked like there were thousands of them but we had the momentum – and finally we broke into a charge. Scousers, not a chance. All they could see was this huge mob looming down over them. They couldn't stop us and suddenly the dual carriageway was full of stampeding Liverpudlians. We ended up running all the way. They split and we marched triumphantly into the city centre. It was the ultimate mob rampage.

Ten days later, we were due to play them at Anfield in the league. We hired a coach, with the intention of heading off for a night out in Blackpool afterwards. All the loonies were on our coach. Unfortunately it was stopped only twenty minutes out of Manchester for being overloaded – plus some enterprising chaps had been upstairs to a pub living quarters and nicked £900-worth of jewellery. We ended up in a Salford police station and missed the game, but still made it out for Blackpool in the evening.

As the night wore on and drink was consumed, we began to look for a club that would let us in. A few of us ended up downstairs in the ex-boxer Brian London's club, the 007. There must have been about twenty of us inside when it dawned on me that there were also Scousers in there. I knew it wouldn't take long to go up.

A pint or two later, I thought, fuck this. I was next to the DJ's box, leaning on a wooden barrier, and could feel the bad atmosphere. They knew, we knew and everyone else in the club knew. They were on one side, we were on the other, with only a couple of birds on the dance floor in between. Someone had to do something, so I started singing the Wembley song.

'Que sera, sera . . .'

Up chirped a few others. We had just got to the first chorus when a pot came whizzing at me. I ducked down on my hands and knees behind this wooden barrier and the place erupted. Glasses, tables and chairs flew across the dance floor, while I was laughing away because I'd caused it. There was no fisticuffs, everyone was just bombing each other.

At the end of my barrier was an exit door. I headed there laughing and gingerly stuck my head out from behind this section to see if things were still being thrown. Then I got up to take the three or four steps to the exit because we wanted to have it in the street. I had taken two steps when, whack, a pint pot hit me on the forehead in the same place as I had been potted three months previously. I was sparko on the floor and someone dragged me out of the exit. As the Scousers tried to get up the stairs and make their way onto the street, the rest of our lads came into the club. It all exploded in the foyer and on the stairs and the Scousers got done in, but by then I was on my way in a cab to Victoria Hospital to get stitched up.

I got back on the coach to go home with blood congealed on my head and stitches sticking out of my forehead. I sat at the front and felt physically sick but the only concern I got from the lads was, 'Shut up you soft cunt, there's fuck all wrong with you.' They were all happy and rowdy because they'd had a fight.

The next day in the *News of the World*, Brian London was giving it the big 'un, saying, 'They've smashed my club up. If they want to fight, put them in the boxing ring with me and I'll take them all on one at a time.' The debate was close between us all about whether we should go back and give it to him, but something must have distracted us, because we never did.

The glass had hit me on a spot I'd been potted previously while out in town on a Saturday night. Four of us were in a bar at about 9pm, literally minding our own business. The shoes, pants, shirt and tie brigade were in there, a stag do or something, and it kicked off, nothing to do with us. The doormen ran around and we stepped aside, but this kid got in my face. I was saying nothing, because it was not football-related and was nothing to do with me. I realised this kid wanted it but he had a pint pot in his right hand, with a handle. I hit him with my right and he went for me. I grabbed him and was pulling him down to get him out of my face when he swung his arm like a fast bowler over the top of his head and brought the pot crashing down on mine, splitting it open.

I somehow got outside, blood leaking from my napper, and soon all the United lads, who were drinking in the Portland Bars, had heard about it.

'O'Neill's been potted!'

They came charging across. The only info they had was that it was the shirt and jacket brigade. From that moment on, everyone around Piccadilly with a jacket on got smashed. Eventually they found the lads involved and one of them was thrown through Lewis's window. It was nothing to do with me, but that's Manchester.

*　　*　　*

FOR THE CUP final against Arsenal, we had another enormous firm. Yet give the Gooners their due; at 10.30am in Covent Garden I was surprised to see a small mob of them come round a corner, a few black lads among them, and were soon over the barriers and at them and would have murdered them if they hadn't run. Some of us carried on chasing and round the corner they had hijacked a milk float. Bottles and crates came at us before they were on their toes again. We couldn't catch them but that set the tone for the day and got everyone up for it.

We got on the tube to go to Wembley and it was full from the first carriage to the last with United thugs and hooligans. I thought, right, Willesden, we'll stop there, because I had this mad idea that Arsenal would be there. We got off and went through the shopping centre, a full train of pissed-up thugs and thieves, and any thought of Arsenal went as the place got pillaged. It was a case of find the jewellers, the old north-west trick. I still wanted the fight but half of this huge mob had other ideas. You could hear the kicking of windows and then see bodies flying over the tills and counters and people running out with God knows what. I just shook my head.

It was a twat of a walk from Willesden to Wembley. By the time we got there I was pissed off and by the end of the game I was even more pissed off. Everyone was in a depression at the result, especially after the way we had come back to 2–2 only for Alan Sunderland to score at the death. I wandered off. I couldn't be arsed talking to people and ended up going back to the same place where the fight had broken out in the morning, thinking United fans would go there, but they didn't. I was leaning on the railing and 350 Arsenal ran round the corner. I thought, you twats. They weren't chasing anyone, they just burst out of the tube station. I was in the right place but there was no-one there and they were all singing. I was gutted.

By 1979, many of our more violent hangers-on had gone. A lot of lads from places like Hull would follow United rather than their hometown team because there was more chance of trouble, but as those opportunities diminished, that element of the Red Army bled away. We were still targets of the authorities, while other firms seemed to be left alone, allowing them to grow and flex their muscles.

For me, the writing was on the wall in an even more dramatic manner. I was nicked for robbery, credit card fraud and a violent fight outside a nightclub. A group of us had met in the Benchill pub on a Friday night for a few drinks and then went to a club in Altrincham. We knew it would probably end in a row because we were leaving Wythenshawe, and that usually meant trouble. No-one wanted it but we knew it would end up that way. We had a good night and didn't know, because we were drunk, that some lads in there wanted to have a go at 'that Wythenshawe lot'. When we came out there was a load of them waiting. It kicked off and we ended up smashing a load of them in, then fucked off. They came after us, we bottled them and we got nicked. Just us, none of them. That's the way it was then; if there was trouble on an estate or in a city, it was always the person from outside who got nicked. So when we left Wythenshawe there was always that danger.

I was banged up in Risley remand centre for six months on the young persons' wing. They had arrested six out of the eight of us, so at least we were together. Four got jail and I got five and a half years for violent disorder and GBH. I shouldn't have got anything like that but I helped this kid out with his story, which put me in the frame more. When the sentence was read out, I couldn't believe it. I hadn't done anything bad enough to warrant five years. To me it was just life: you got involved in things. My thought was, I've got Manchester United to watch, you can't do this to me!

But that wasn't all. I was also up for credit card fraud to run concurrent, and robbery. The latter charge related to the theft of wages from Smiths Crisps. I had waited for the feller with the money, grabbed the bag, he fell over and I went back to the estate with £2,600. The police came round and someone on the estate had seen me getting out of the stolen car and had identified me. As for the credit card, I didn't know what I was doing as my head had gone at the time. I would end up serving three and a half years of my sentence.

* * *

THEY TOOK ME by taxi from Minshull Street Crown Court in Manchester to HMP Walton in Liverpool. Walton was where

157

you went if you got over five years, which was classed as a long sentence. I was twenty-one years old and, yes, a football hooligan, but not a hardened criminal. This was alien territory for me.

When I walked into Walton I thought it was Alcatraz. This was a man's jail. The first person I saw was the boxer John Conteh's brother in reception, a tough-looking half-caste. The rooms and corridors were all dimmed yellow lights and just awful. Walton was built in Victorian times. It had gallows for executions by the famous hangman Albert Pierrepoint until the last person was hanged there in 1964. It was supposed to hold under 900 prisoners but always had a lot more, meaning it was overcrowded and understaffed.

I ended up on H Wing for thirteen months. It was the only place in the north-west for long-term prisoners. H Wing had one of the most brutal regimes imaginable. You had no luxuries and were in the cell for twenty-three hours a day. If it looked like rain, you didn't get your one-hour exercise – and when you did you walked round in a circle. There could be ten or eleven days at a time when you didn't get out of your cell except to go down four at a time to get your dinner and your tea. It was the screws versus the cons. Slopping out, shitting in your cell. Horrible.

I was the young kid on the wing and any time that door opened I was out and running around. I met all the characters who were major criminals or vicious and I didn't have a problem with any of them. There was John Molloy, who was part of the Carl Bridgewater paperboy murder trial. Then there was Barry McKie, a Scouse half-caste kid who was a real character and who eventually escaped from custody on a coach. I would meet him again years later in Sudbury Prison, where he was finishing off a life sentence. The main man on the wing was Tommy Comerford. 'Tacker', as they called him, was a legendary drug smuggler: heroin, cocaine, cannabis, you name it, he imported it. He was a fat Scouse bloke who had a pub in the Dock Road area and told funny stories. Comerford didn't give a fuck. Even the screws looked on him as the major criminal, but he was a jolly chap.

I ended up on three sitdown protests because I was daft as a brush and Barry McKie and all his cohorts decided this was what we had to do because we didn't get any exercise. The only people who won were the screws – they were all on overtime. They should have steamed us but the governor wanted to play it softly-softly. We would all sit down outside but by night-time people would be running indoors because it was so cold. The screws wanted us to stay out because they were on treble time and being called in from different jails.

I saw people being dragged down metal staircases with their heads bashing off the steps. I saw screws kicking fuck out of people. My wing had the Block downstairs, where they put you in solitary for serious misdemeanours, and they were kicking fuck out of people on a regular basis and everyone knew it. But you knew where you stood, which I actually found more acceptable than the regimes now. Any man can adapt to any situation; you develop a tolerance to it. You learn to understand where you are and to deal with it. I preferred that to regimes I later experienced because all cons do now is whinge. They are constantly crying about where their mail is, can they use the phone. In those days, if you opened your mouth to the screws you got leathered. You didn't ask for anything because you got nothing.

The old lags loved the stories I told them about the football. They thought I was off my head because it was not their world. They were all criminals while I just thought I was one of the lads, even though I had been convicted of criminal activity. I even met one of the Scouse blokes who had done the forged tickets for the 1976 Cup final. There was no such thing as association. I only ever went in someone else's cell once or twice. You had no freedom. The door was shut and that was it. It was vicious but not towards each other.

After thirteen months they sent me to the lunatic asylum

known as Wakefield Prison. It housed the nuttiest people in the land. I was surrounded by sex cases, psycho murderers, perverts and nutters of every description. When I arrived, the serial killer Robert Maudsley, who was later called Britain's Hannibal Lecter, had not long murdered two men in one afternoon *inside* the prison. Maudsley cut open the head of one of his victims with a homemade knife and ate his brains. You can imagine how happy I was to find out he was still in there – and I was to be on the same block, though he was in solitary confinement. That was one of the first tales they told me.

I acted the young thug, as if to say, if anyone fucks with me they are going to have it. It seemed to work. I also kept myself busy running around, getting into things like dealing tobacco. I also completed a tailoring course while I was in there and I ended up designing and making a hand-made suit, stitched it myself, lining, the lot. I made a big overcoat as well. That was the only sane relief I got.

Fortunately I was in a single cell, but I didn't understand how to be in a single cell because I wanted someone to talk to, being so young. No-one was isolated from the sex cases because they were in the majority. The worst rapists in the country. Yet it didn't go off in there much. It was fucking weird. I teamed up with two ex-soldiers who had killed someone and dropped them in a lake in Stafford: Jimmy and Macca. Come the weekend we would run round the shale football pitch doing forty laps and that helped keep me sane as well.

I did twenty-eight days in the segregation unit at Wakefield. It was for money laundering and acting as a 'tobacco baron'. You were left in the cell alone and every morning the door opened and you had to stand up. The Governor might appear and ask, 'Everything all right?' and before you had time to answer, the door would shut. Same with the doctor.

To make things worse, I was missing a lot of footie action. This period was the start of the so-called 'casual' fashion –

something I'll return to – and new faces were replacing some of the dinosaurs of the past. We also still had a great contingent of barmies, and when they went on one it was a case of burn, destroy, wreck and kill. Nothing could hold them.

One of the trips where the barmies and the lads both earned their spurs was a full-on encounter at Ayresome Park in the 1979–80 season. As I was residing at Her Majesty's Pleasure at the time I have to thank *Red Issue* fanzine for letting me reproduce this account from one of the lads.

When we talk about the Cockneys and Leeds being achingly slow to get into the casual scene, can you imagine how far behind the north-east was? A trip up there is an unattractive prospect at the best of times. On the plus side, you were always guaranteed a marauding mob of some description, as you were taking on punks, skinheads, kids with beer bellies in football shirts. A real mishmash.

It was a serious arse for a game no one was really bothered about, so much so it was decided, sod it, we'll go on the special, as to take service trains you had to change at Leeds and York. No one had taken the special for a couple of years and the week of the game, someone thought, hang on, we don't do specials any more. We're past all that. Half a dozen coaches were booked in no time flat but with no mobile phones loads of kids were unaware of developments.

I got to Victoria on the day to meet the firm for the special but there were only about 100 there. 'What the fuck's gone on?' Everyone knew we were turning out for this one. 'It's odd. Everyone must have jibbed it.' As we were getting ready to board, two lads came flying in. They relayed the story of the coaches, and how the word had supposedly been sent round but it was too late to do anything about it as they'd already left.

So there we were: on the special like good children. After an eternity best forgotten, we reached Middlesbrough, where two Transit vans of our lads had parked up waiting. They'd heard the mob had plotted up at a pub on the outskirts and were marching in. Pre-mobile days, we had no chance of finding them.

We headed into town. When you went to Ayresome Park from the station, you had to go through the centre proper. We met a little resistance straight away, perhaps thirty or forty. They got chased in no time and we made our way to the ground. We didn't settle in a pub, as in staying on the move we might just bump into the others. Once near the ground, however, we bowled into the first pub and within half an hour it had cleared of locals, who realised we weren't the friendliest of fans.

As the afternoon wore on, people who used the pub every game started turning up. They weren't impressed and inevitably there was friction. It wasn't long before a Boro fan said the wrong thing to someone in the bogs and bang, he was gone. One of his mates came out and announced his pal had been lamped by a Man United fan, presumably so he'd get lots of backup. Wrong. We were up and out of our chairs and into them. Cue lunacy all over. Punches traded, Boro fans slung over the bar and everything. Prolonged aggro wasn't on the cards as the landlord summoned the Old Bill.

It was roughly 2pm and we headed up towards the ground. It wasn't very long before we bumped a mob of eighty-odd Boro, still in the skinhead, Dr Marten phase. You could see them looking at us like we were off another planet. I think we were there before the Scousers that season and so this was their first sight of a casual firm. They weren't given long before we were into them. They did have a proper go these lads; they were in the main a lot older than us but despite being very much the younger element of our firm at that time, most of us could more than handle ourselves and these Boro realised that they were facing a brick wall. A few were down on their arses and we backed them across the road before they evaporated down an alley on the far side.

We got picked up by the police, taken to the ground and penned there, where we drew the locals' attention: 'What's with all them clothes and trainers? You look like poofs.' We treated this with the disdain it deserved. There were at least 3–400 Boro in this street, all of them getting excited, the police were definitely wobbling but we were going nowhere. They were a mob of all-comers. Punks, skinheads, Docs, donkey jackets, some of them even had braces. The saddest part was, even as they abused us for not wearing colours of any kind, you knew that one day, when they finally cottoned on, they would end up looking like us.

A big lump came across the road to give us some abuse as to our attire and demeanour. If only he could have looked irony up in the dictionary before he left. Picture him, 6'4", half-mast jeans, braces, skinhead, Ben Sherman, polished up cherry red Docs. 'I want a fucking word with you lot,' like he was going to take us all on. Even the OB looked at his posturing and laughed. 'You think you're something after that ruck earlier. You've turned up here in your supposedly smart clothes; well I think you look like a load of queers. You look stupid with your daft haircuts and anyway, you're shitbags, because you've got no colours on. We've noted who you are. You came off the station as a mob and we know you've got to go back there and you're going to be well outnumbered.'

What he didn't know of course was that somewhere out there were 300 of our finest. Either way, we were unconcerned with his threats and he got fobbed off in a wonderfully condescending manner, 'Yeah, yeah, we'll see you later on the main street and sort it.' We weren't unduly concerned but Middlesbrough was generally uncharted waters. The one thing we did know was if it got naughty, you could end up with a full barmy army on your case. This big parcel was still going on with himself and all the while there's a growing disturbance down the street as Boro fans ran for cover.

One of the lads interrupted. 'You're not dealing with a hundred and forty anymore. Take a look at what's coming up behind you.'

Over his shoulder, the approaching disturbance in the street erupted. The road that had been packed with self-styled threatening Boro fans had opened right up and we could see our firm marching down the middle driving locals before them. This drew the attention of our police escort and they've all gone flying off. Straight away someone banged the parcel. The blow wobbled him and I think he took a kick that sent him flying. He scrambled to his feet and ran headlong into the mass of fleeing Boro fans, who'd ended up charging back towards us.

United's main firm ended up in the middle of the road, with Boro ranked on both pavements, staring open mouthed. 140 of us had been enough to create a stir, this 300 was even better. They'd skittled Boro all round the back of their main stand and past the away end. It was one of those moments that you never forget. They walked up to us cocky as fuck, blanking the insults thrown from the locals. As the two halves of the firm mingled to swap tales, one lad came up, arms out to emphasise his point: 'How good are we? How fucking good are we? Isn't this the gaff where the whole ground will turn on you and send you home done in with a flea in your ear? What a load of bollocks. We've just taken the absolute piss there, skittled the whole street everywhere.

'We chased them everywhere. Then we came round the corner near the away end, and they've all got their backs to us. A few digs were swapped and then we were right into them. I was pissing myself as we went through them. It wasn't the fact they were backing away, it was the looks on their faces as they did. You could see them thinking, what are these lot all about?'

It must have been a strange sight at the time. All these lads with smart haircuts and nice clothes, every one of them game as fuck. It completely threw the locals.

United fans were by now piling in the turnstiles but the amount of local sightseers was unbelievable. You could see people pointing at us. One Boro lad came over and tapped a mate: 'I don't want no trouble but what's all this clobber you've got on?' We all had Pods and Kickers and the like. 'What is it all about?'

'It's just something that's taken off in Manchester and dare I say it Liverpool as well. I don't know if the Scousers have been here yet but they'll all have it on. City will too, but there won't be that many of them.'

What a shit ground Ayresome Park was. For those who don't remember, you used to get a corner of the ground. They used to sing 'Ayresome Boot Boys' to some Sham 69 tune. 'Ayresome boys, Ayresome boys, laced up boots and corduroys.' It tells you what level they were at.

Some of these Ayresome Boot Boys, perhaps ten, had paid in the United end, which was a game thing to do. They were in the bottom corner. I think Boro went one up, and they jumped up and cheered. All their skinheads were in a paddock next to us, so all they had to do was cheer and then climb over the wall separating us. It would have worked sweetly for them if Fate had smiled kindly.

She didn't. Six or seven of the lads had nipped to the loo and were on their way back right past this little team. As soon as they jumped up for the goal, our lads went into them. That thwarted their escape plan and we all pummelled the living daylights out of them. They were rescued by the OB, and I'll always remember seeing Doc Martens in the air as the police pushed them headfirst over the wall.

That revved the whole atmosphere up. Word had obviously gone round that there was a strange-looking service mob about, which also gave things an edge. The match itself was a boring game of bollocks despite the 2–2 scoreline. Boro were giving it the big 'un outside. The whole street was full of them, hundreds, topped up with the swell of the passing crowd. It did look like an army. We were getting ourselves together, but the first thing that needed sorting was this: 140 would be going one way to the train while 300 were heading back to the buses. We decided to all go to the station and rely on the police to bring the coaches so they could get rid of us.

So there we were, listening to these cunts going on like they can't get us out there quick enough. What did they think we were going to do, stay in there pissing our pants? There was a main gate, with a little one either side. Some barmies started kicking the big double gates. That wasn't our style. We preferred to get out, mingle with the crowd, sort ourselves and then do things professionally. For some reason though, we all got on it and charged the gate, battering to get the police to open it. We had a 2,400 following that day, and it was still a ground decent fans didn't go to, so the bulk were barmies. They were all mad for it and there was a huge surge of United fans pushing on the gate. It was dodgy, we could hardly breathe.

The gate had two metal girders at the top and two at the

bottom that fitted in to the brickwork either side. It could have been there since the Great War. I heard a strange noise and watched as the top of the gate folded away outwards. The wall started to crumble and then it wasn't there anymore. The whole wall fell away in a cloud of dust. The dibble were straight in, battering us with truncheons to back us off though we really didn't have anywhere to go. They were saying there were people under the rubble, which no-one took seriously. They opened the side gates and we were out and that was it. No messing, everyone was straight into this waiting mob. It was only a narrow street and that produced proper close toe-to-toe fighting. We backed them off both ways up the road. Our barmies got stuck in too and make no mistake some of them could have a go. This Boro mob got battered right off. There might have been 500 of them slavering outside for us to come out, but 2,000 Reds emerged revved up.

The police gradually established control and calmed the barmies. We clicked into autopilot and slithered through the crowd to head into town. We moved for perhaps half a mile and then found the main road back into town. Boro had regrouped and got ahead of us. Hordes came at us on a mad charge and I mean hordes. Five, possibly six hundred. We held our line and our nerve and counter charged when they'd closed to less than twenty yards. This was a big-time battle, serious close-quarter fighting, none of this charging about. A week-in week-out team of 400 is worth three times that number who don't know each other. This Boro mob had perhaps a team of 150 in the middle holding it together. The rest were largely hangers-on. Once the central firm broke, the rest swiftly followed. We pursued them down the street for a good while but they all split off down side streets and alleys.

Orders were shouted. 'Don't peel off and chase, stick

together.' You can imagine the fate that would have befallen a little team who split off. They might not have had the quality required, but the locals were definitely game.

We neared the top of the street, wanting to do a left and head into town. As we got there, the police turned up from everywhere in a seriously tense state. They'd not had a good day. Some of our barmies were still going mental, smashing cars and the like. The OB held us there surrounded. They tried to herd us off to the station but a few of the coach kids were reluctant to go. As part of the smaller train party, I didn't like the sound of this, as splitting up didn't make sense. The OB were only too delighted to have a reason to split us in two. Some lads suggested we squeeze on the coaches but we wanted to make sure everyone who came on the train got back okay.

'Fuck it, you go back to the coaches, that's how you came. We're on the rattler and we're going home on it.'

'Come with us, it's done and dusted here.'

'No it ain't. Cozzers or not, they'll come again on that shopping precinct. Once they get the scent two-thirds of us have gone, they'll really fancy the job.'

The OB had had enough and ushered us in our respective directions. We had to forget the others, they weren't there anymore. The bulk of the police went with them too. So, about 140 strong again, we set off for town. We could see it coming, glimpses down side streets, behind shops, the Boro mob building up into something decent. We knew the only way out. Whatever happened, no one would budge. Over half of us were twenty or under. Most Boro looked like blokes. I could even sense the OB with us wobbling. I, for one, thought we were definitely getting it. The moment this 400–500 Boro moved, the dibble were going to melt.

Policing being as it was, we just ambled on to our apparent doom.

We drew level with Woolworth's and then they came, Zulu fashion. From the front, the left and the right; it was quite nicely done for such throwbacks. Stand and have it is the drill. I was just drawing breath to give it a big 'stand' when bang, I copped for a big lump of wood right across the front of my head. I still carry the scar – and a bump. I was right on the front line and they'd come out of Woolworth's fifteen-handed. A nice surprise manoeuvre which wobbled me, but instead of pressing the advantage he brandished his stick and that was all the time I needed. I grabbed him, we tussled and I realised why he was a stick man. He couldn't or wouldn't fight, throwing no punches in his attempts to escape my grasp. I had hold of his hair, battering him against the pavement. They were piling all over us and if we'd weakened, we'd have been overrun. Fair play to all concerned, no one budged. Everyone traded blows. Young we may have been, but we were largely lads of good reputation. Credit was due to this little firm from Blackley who could have it with anyone, they held us together. They were right into them, no messing. You didn't get it very often, but we were even rolling round on the floor grappling with them.

We had one bloke with us who'd been notable at Anfield in years previous. He was a fringe player, rarely got involved but he was a right hard cunt. I never even knew what part of Manchester he was from but I remember thinking he was rum as fuck. He was an island, immovable, getting stuck right in. People like that were the required material as this ruck went on and on. The only thing that finally broke it up was everyone needing a breather. We'd still be at it now, I swear. I regained my feet, and we got ourselves together and went on a charge right at them. Then OB reinforcements showed up. We went on one last mad charge and scattered some down the side street before the dibble established control.

We had to give them their due, they were game. Okay, they had 3–1 odds in their favour, but they stood and had it when we shocked them and held our ground. The police gathered us up and we continued on our way. Close to the station, Boro came on one last charge, about 500 of them. The sky went black for a bit with a hail of bricks and bottles, and we made an attempt to break through police lines but the OB had it sorted so it was all to no avail.

A couple of Boro came over. 'Fair play, you stood outnumbered. Most teams that come here don't fucking reign if there's not enough of them.' There were the usual clothes enquiries. We weren't bigging ourselves up, you knew these yokels couldn't help but be impressed.

'This is our thing now. You don't want to be recognised, you don't wear colours. You can move about in foreign towns and no one connects you to football. Once you're away you're away. Then you can graft.'

'Graft, what's graft?'

'Graft, money-getting, readies, cash.'

He didn't grasp the concept, so we switched off. The land that time forgot it most definitely was, and we were all glad of getting home. At least the locals had had a proper go, and as a functioning casual mob, we had made a decent first impression.

What you have to remember about Middlesbrough is that they're all mutants up there. They'd fight anybody and anything and very few teams would take big numbers there to have a crack at them. Having said that, the only time I saw them at Old Trafford in that era was when about 150 of them got off at Victoria and were marched straight to the ground. United shadowed them all along Chester Road. They were the ugliest, scruffiest mob I've ever seen, but they looked like they could have a fight.

An even bigger day I missed was Elland Road on May 3, 1980. It was the day we could have won the league and we took 15,000. For weeks we had been singing a new song:

> *Hark now hear United sing*
> *The Scousers ran away*
> *And there will be a massacre*
> *Upon the Third of May*

History records that we blew it again and the title went to Liverpool, who were at Villa Park. You can imagine the reaction at Elland Road; at one stage one of my brothers was on an embankment outside hitting them with a spade. United had the Lowfield, the side that stretched from the Gelderd End to the South Stand. Their boys went in the South Stand in those days and all game United were jumping over into it and kicking off.

During this period we also took what many say was the biggest mob we ever had at a London game. West Ham had been getting a name for themselves with their Inter City Firm, so United were determined to put them in their place. Our mob met somewhere they had never met before or since – Stratford, in East London – and Mick Grogan, a great friend of mine from Wigan, led them to Upton Park. He marched an army estimated to be 700-strong through the streets. Apparently it's a four- or five-mile walk and the mob stretched back over a mile. And the maddest thing about it was they had no police escort.

They came up from the market side at West Ham and rampaged down the street. Some West Ham came out of a pub at first, not realising the size of United's army, and then it was just a full sweep of the street. Some West Ham were even taking photographs of them. They carried on and carried on and went all around the ground unopposed. When some West Ham did show at the corner of the Queens pub, they were blitzed. We ran them round and round the market. They must have known United were coming as they'd marched for miles, so they can't say we took them unawares.

I heard the story while I was in jail and was going off my head that I'd missed it. Apparently we took liberties all over. So you can imagine a few of the lads were a little bit puzzled when a West Ham book came out years later with their version of events: that twenty Hammers came out of a pub and stood off the whole of the United firm while the rest of their boys got together – 'and then we gave it to 'em.' That's what it says. So twenty of them stood off 700 of United's main firm, did they? They really are supermen. Is there anyone out there who actually believes this bullshit?

Another comprehensive victory over a London firm came at home against Arsenal's Gooners, but not after they – and others – had first given us a shock at their place. Over to the kid from *Red Issue* fanzine again:

In 1981 everyone went on the train to Euston. There were always lads travelling about on various grafts in various parts of the country and so there were about fifty of the firm already waiting for us, a common occurrence. We wandered over to a pub in King's Cross where we'd arranged to meet perhaps seventy Cockney Reds. Instead of taking the underground straight to Highbury, we went further up the line to Turnpike Lane. We'd not been there an hour when it was time to swerve the dibble again, so it was back on the underground. One stop back to Manor House Park, out the side entrance and around through the streets to the ground from a hopefully unexpected direction.

There was a definite drinking zone in those days where

the Gooners went boozing before the game, and we plotted up there. Arsenal came and had a go and to be fair they did make quite a decent showing, but they lacked both the quality and quantity to deal with United. They broke and ran after a short engagement but continually emerged in teams from side streets as we marched on Highbury. There were further little offs, as it's tight round Highbury, and whilst nothing came at us en masse, there was a lot of friction with the locals as we moved through.

Post-match is a different story. What happened to the firm I must relate secondhand. As a result of something four of us had spotted the season previous, we spewed going with the firm. It had been nothing special before-hand, and there was no reason to think it would be anything different after. We did enough rowing up and down the country every week and instead nipped off to take care of some business. We didn't find out about events till the following week.

United moved off from Highbury looking for Arsenal's mob, perhaps 300 strong. A hundred or so had been split off by the police and escorted to the tube back to Euston. As United moved down Highbury Hill they bumped into Arsenal's firm. For the first time a decent United firm, decent not just in numbers but composition, really came up against it. On sighting the enemy, United moved to engage. Arsenal really came at them though, and they were up for it. Far gamer, in fact, than anyone could credit. Cockneys just kept piling in the street and the 300 United were swiftly encircled and ultimately overpowered. People were going down all over, it was a seriously violent punch-up as some of our best gave as good as they could in the circumstances.

Afterwards no one could work out how Arsenal had put on such a show. Not only had they been psyched up, but they'd never previously been able to turn out 6–700 lads. Thankfully the dibble appeared and split everything up. United were scraped up and bundled off to Holloway Road tube station and on to Euston. The hundred couldn't believe their eyes when they saw them. It was the worst pasting anyone could remember and everyone was devastated. As was remarked at the time, 'I don't know how they were that good today, it was like taking half of North London on.'

That was a lot closer to the truth than anyone realised. The many questions were answered by a phone call off the Cockney Reds. Contingents from Millwall, Chelsea, West Ham and a bigger mob than all three combined of Tottenham had joined up with the Gunners (the North London rivalry being nothing like as intense twenty years ago). The clubs we met regularly had had enough of suffering at United's hands, and were sick of our immaculate reputation. It was the hoolie equivalent of the Anything But United phenomenon the team experienced in the Nineties. Obviously, it wasn't all of the lads from these other clubs, nothing like, but the extra fifty here, 200 there, had made the difference. That doesn't change the basic facts though. A decent-sized United firm had had a proper slap off an even more decent-sized mob of cockneys.

The full story came out over the following months. Spurs were first in, and then they brought West Ham. West Ham knew some Millwall and so they were signed on and so on. They weren't all on the best of terms, but they could hold it together for the out without it dissolving into inter-cockney squabbling.

The general mood was, 'Those cockneys have taken liberties. It happened at Highbury, so we'll make Arsenal pay for it first and do a proper job on them.' Obviously we couldn't reassemble the cockney alliance in once place to dismember them, so we had to settle for taking them one at a time. West Ham and Millwall were both lower league at that point, so we couldn't have it with them in the normal course of events anyway.

The home game of the 1981–82 season. United were in the Salisbury and half a dozen other drinking establishments within easy reach of Oxford Road station. The police used to change tactics and their swerve at that time was to shift cockneys arriving at Piccadilly by any train available to Oxford Road and change there onto one of the trains that ferried fans to Old Trafford railway station. We were well onto this manoeuvre and so the vast majority of our forces were covering the approaches to the station, ready to go at a moment's notice.

Every preparation had been made, but fate smiled on us that day just to give it that little extra. Not long before Arsenal arrived at Piccadilly, perhaps seventy Stoke City had come off a train and walked to Victoria, bound for some no-mark outfit in Lancashire I presume. Aptly, somewhere around Balloon Street, they'd walked into fifty or so United heading to join the mobilization around Oxford Road and it had gone straight off. It might have deprived us of fifty good lads, but that ruck drew the majority of the police looking after Arsenal away from Piccadilly just as they were putting the cockneys on a rattler to Oxford Road. They had a mere five coppers with them, not so much for protection as to make sure they didn't miss the stop and end up in Knutsford. A decent firm would have easily given the OB the slip as soon as they'd stepped off the first train. Arsenal were a joke though and would have quite meekly got on the train to OT. As it turned out, they never had a choice in the matter.

Four kids with an older lad in a car had been dispatched

to Piccadilly as scouts. As soon as they spotted Arsenal moving between platforms they dived back in the motor and drove to Oxford Road. The word went round to get ready. The same scouts then went in the station to clock the Gooners' train coming in. They positioned themselves at the start of the platform so they could see the first few right away. Arsenal pulled in on platform 2. The two kids on the platform called to the two kids sat on the wall. They shouted down to the mob poised at the bottom of the stairs and we steamed into the station, 500 strong.

Everything had been worked out in advance. They couldn't come in on 4, that was for trains into town. They were unlikely to come in on 5 as that line ends in Oxford Road. They had to come in on 3, 2 or less likely 1 and we knew how we'd approach that scenario before we'd moved from the pub.

United charged in, up the steps and over the bridge that links the platforms and poured down. Half of us went straight for them, the other half swept down on to platform 1 and across the tracks to come from the other side.

Arsenal were only 200-handed and never had the quality, so it was a walkover. I'll never forget a Gooner in a Burberry coat bailing off the train, brandishing his umbrella and stopping dead as he saw what was coming. United were coming from three sides by now, as the press of bodies on the stairs to go over the platforms meant some lads had just taken the direct route across the tracks from 4 to 3 and 2.

The train driver, out. The five coppers, out, screaming for reinforcements. Arsenal wouldn't get off the train; they were cringing on the seats. Their main lad had a go to be fair, and got absolutely battered against the side of the carriage. Arsenal wouldn't do the decent thing and get off the rattler so we had to go in and get them. Total carnage.

They sought escape by diving on to the tracks and were generally pushed out by the weight of bodies on board and into the howling mob on the track that side. There was no refuge on Oxford Road that day, we were too hungry, too numerous and too organised.

Picture then the scene. An abandoned train smashed to pieces; a busy city centre train station deserted by all travelling civilians. No police, no cameras, just 700 lads fighting on platform, train and track. In retrospect, they must have turned the lines off and held all the trains up but at the time everyone was locked too deeply into the frenzy to pay heed to the fact they were on a main line. Total chaos. I remember thinking at the time that this is how the end of the world will sound.

The police were none too keen to come and split it up and chose the more sensible option of letting the storm blow itself out. They finally came in cautiously. It would give you pause for thought when 500 handy lads had just performed a textbook three-pronged ambush Hannibal would have been proud of.

The next season, thirty Arsenal tried to sign on with United at Spurs. They got spewed, but their testimonial that day said it all. 'That was some hiding you gave us at Oxford Road. We've got ultimate respect. All right, it was on your own manor but the ferocity was overwhelming. We had some proper fellers there who've been up against it before, but it was too much. We just crumbled.'

* * *

THERE WERE SOME events that I was glad I missed while I was inside. One was a tragedy that should never have happened. As I was not there I cannot comment much but it would be a cop-out not to mention it.

In 1982 we played Tottenham at White Hart Lane. As usual, it was going off all day, proper rucking on the streets. They trailed United to Seven Sisters tube station and stormed in to attack them for one last time. I believe about 250 United were at the bottom of the escalator and Tottenham were at the top. There was a clash and a lot of confusion and apparently someone pressed the emergency stop button on the escalator. This brought it to an abrupt halt and people fell in a heap. One man, a Tottenham fan, was trapped in the crush and died, while others were injured.

Little Dessie: *We came down Seven Sisters, trouble all the way, and for once peeled off and came in at the other side of the Underground station, while most of the United were on the entrance opposite. The next thing it has just gone. We were on the escalator, they were above us and there was fighting. Later on we were led to believe that someone had pressed the button and one lad has come right over the top of everyone and flattened people like skittles, then there has been a crush. A saw one girl, a punk, with her hair actually stuck in the escalator. She was okay though.*

It was chaotic. We got back to Euston and I know it sounds silly, but we were playing blind man's buff in the carriage. That's how daft we were. We had no idea of the seriousness of it. But when we reached Macclesfield I noticed a few cops on the platform, Wilmslow, a few more. By the time we reached Piccadilly they were everywhere. The only lads they were after were those with dark skin. Coco and Fez were pulled straight away but the rest of us just got off.

The following Monday I was sat in my house at night when there was a knock on the door. 'Little Des?' the guy said when I answered. I soon found out you don't fuck about with the Murder Squad. But they had put two and two together and got five.

Black Sam in London had gone abroad after the game – something we often did on those days to make an earner. They decided he had gone on the run and so eventually they pulled him in and charged him over the lad's death. But he had not done it and the charges were dropped.

There was another near-tragedy in the same year that was quite definitely deliberate. In September 1982, Everton did one of their dirtiest tricks and carved up a United fan called Jobe Henry so badly that he needed 200 stitches to put his back together again. Everton had done their usual stunt by this time: they hadn't shown before the game, then afterwards United went looking for them but nobody could find their mob. After a while everyone began to drift off to the pub. Then they came out of the woodwork, a mob of about 200 of them. I must admit, they had it sussed. They had come out of the ground, gone over Trafford Bridge, down Trafford Road and then sneaked back through onto East Ordsall Lane and back on to Chapel Street and then to Victoria Station. Avoid the main United mobs, happy days. On the way they sussed Jobe and cut him up. Some game local kids came off the Ordsall estate to fight them and then they sneaked off to the station. We later found out they had used that route a couple of times before. What is the point of coming with a firm if you are going to sneak off?

On a slightly different note, one incident that made me chuckle while I was inside was reading a short newspaper report of an fight at Euston when United played Liverpool in the Charity Shield:

Boxer jailed

A professional boxer from Salford was jailed for three months for leading "a disorderly rabble" of fellow Manchester United supporters.

Clerkenwell Magistrates Mr Mark Romer said the

Euston Station area had become "an all too familiar battle-ground" for rival fans and courts had to take a tough line.

Paul Doyle, aged 25, of Clarence Street, admitted using threatening behaviour after the Charity Shield match at Wembley when he led a charge towards Liverpool fans.

The report should have mentioned Doyley's nickname: 'One Punch', because he could flatten anyone he hit. He's one of Manchester's hardest men and I almost felt sorry for any Scousers who got in his way that day. Almost.

* * *

FOOTBALL HAD KEPT me going inside. The arguments we used to have were unreal. If United were getting beat it was like the whole wing was on my case. For the last two months of my sentence, I applied to go back to Manchester because I didn't want to get on anyone's nerves talking about getting out when I was in with lifers. Your conversation changes when you're about to be freed. I got the okay and soon saw some familiar faces in Strangeways, lads off the estate and from all different parts of Manchester. Compared to where I had been, Strangeways was a stupid, shouting, bawling, juvenile gaff, but it allowed me to get back in the swing of more 'normal' life.

I was full of anger at people outside who had shat on me and people inside at how I had been locked up. All I wanted to do was get out and have a fight at the match. I was going mad in my head, playing it all over in my mind, things where I thought people had wronged me and I was going to have them. Yet the moment I walked out of that old door there and into the street, the anger went. It was like a big mad weight lifting off my head or dropping straight through my body and taking everything out of me.

One of my best pals at the time was Derek Whittaker. As I stood at the gate waiting to go out, the big doors were open and a prison van was going in. Unbeknown to me, Derek was inside it banging on the window. One of the people I most wanted to see was going inside.

I was depressed for two weeks. My first night out was weird; everyone was drunk and I was sober as a judge in town, even though I was in the pub from 7pm. It took me a fortnight to get properly drunk. Prison didn't change me though. I got my personality back and got straight into the football, but it took me a while to understand what was going on. I soon found out that things had changed.

CHAPTER ELEVEN

REBUILDING THE FIRM

OUR ESTATE WAS different when I came out of jail. Everyone was on the dole. Heroin had appeared, insidiously. Crime was rising, cash was tight and a lot of people seemed to have no hope. It was not an optimistic time. I didn't know what I was going to do. I'd never had any thought of a career and I had no money. My only ambition was to watch United and I thought it would carry on the same way. There was no-one to discuss anything with. I ended up hod-carrying after three weeks, signing on the dole at the same time, and got a flat in Wythenshawe opposite my new boozer, the Greenwood Tree.

I also encountered a lot of new faces on the football scene, young lads I didn't recognise. Some of the older faces had drifted away. Jeff Lewis rarely got involved any more and pretty much packed it up after a City game when some silly little twat stabbed him. Others you would see only on special occasions or bump into by accident. Their lives had changed; they had married, had kids and lumbered themselves with mortgages. But I hadn't changed.

Local scallies off the estates were also following United abroad in pre-season, using Persil tickets for cheap travel, or watching England, mainly for thieving. The Collyhurst lot had been doing this for years – they would thieve on the ferry, on the train, anywhere – but now lots of others were following suit. I had missed the boat a bit but watching England was not my thing anyway. Apparently the Cockneys resented United's presence at England games and there was a story at Luxembourg that they had ganged up to attack United and some West ham geezer was waving an axe about.

The biggest change of all on the terraces was the arrival of the 'casuals'. There had been inklings of this before I was sent down, with straight jeans, training shoes and Slazenger jumpers beginning to spread. When I came out, it was everywhere. In fact it had been around so long by then that flares were coming back in! Now to me, someone who had spent the whole of the Seventies involved in mass brawls with skinheads, bootboys, suedeheads, Clockwork Orange nutters and punks, and who had just come out of two of the hardest prisons in Britain, casuals was a numpty, embarrassing word. I imagine it came from some woolyback, some college graduate. What's a casual? You are what you are and you wear what you wear.

I admit it passed me by – there's not much call for such fashion among the mental cases in Wakefield Prison – and I looked on it with a bit of scorn. I also thought its origins were a bit of a media myth. Scousers go on about how they started this fashion but the fuckers have been wearing tracksuits, trainers and parkas since God knows when. I was called a tramp if I wore a parka at school. I wore a duffel coat because it was practical and had a big hood – and then found that even they had become trendy!

Many people had stopped wearing scarves by 1977 so they could mingle. The whole idea was to try to infiltrate your opponents as they were being marched to the ground or through the city centre, so suddenly wearing scarves was bollocks. People also stopped wearing scarves so they wouldn't get their heads kicked in. Suddenly people were going to the match in normal clothes, rather than lit up like Christmas trees. But that was hardly a fashion.

I don't want to go to the match in designer clothes. Everybody who knows me knows I have never gone in for that. It was an attempt to be a cool-looking firm, but if these people go out and buy designer clothes they are not going to get stuck right in and be swung about and have beer spilled on them. I'm expecting to be rolling about the floor. I'm expecting my coat to be ripped. I'm not going on a catwalk, am I? I'm going to put my life in danger.

* * *

ONE OF MY first games back was Chelsea at home and it gave me a chance to put my stamp back on the firm. Chelsea had just been promoted again and as usual thought they were London's gift to the hooligan world. They'd all been skinheads when I went to jail but now they were in diamond Pringles like all the rest. We're hard, we're stylish, we're mad, we're Chelsea. Big deal.

Nothing happened before the game, as usual: when do these Cockney firms ever come into town and have it? Afterwards, the area around the ground was packed. I took up position by the shops on Chester Road with my mate Mally. Chelsea eventually came up what is now Sir Matt Busby Way and there was no noise, no singing or shouting. There was a lot of unease and electricity in the air, people waiting to see what was going to happen. But I was blazing inside, ready to explode.

When they hit the junction of Warwick Road, this firm of Chelsea split away and turned right down Chester Road – right past where I was waiting. They walked down the middle of the street with their main faces at the front, sporting their meanest stares. They must have been so hyped up that they didn't notice me standing in the shadows behind a roadside crash barrier to their right.

As they walked past, I leaped the barrier. Their boys at the front were still concentrating so hard that they paid me no attention and I'm sure some of them thought I was one of their mob, jumping over to join them, as I was on my own. How wrong can you be? A firm of United gathered around a bus stop on the other side of Chester Road had noticed this split-away mob and began to fan out, preparing to take them on. Chelsea drew to a stop, considering their next move – and that was when I made *my* move.

I smashed my right fist into the nearest lad's face. He dropped like a stone. I moved a few paces forward, to the front of their mob, and banged another one. He went down too.

United charged. As the Chelsea back-pedalled, I jumped back over the barrier to avoid getting trampled by my own boys. I rejoined Mally and we sauntered off, caught the first bus and laughed all the way into town.

* * *

SOMETIMES MY SEVENTIES mentality was not right for the occasion, though. When I came out I was still the same age in my head as when I'd gone in, and still as mad as a hatter. We played Everton at home and instead of going around town first, I went to the ground, watching what was going on. It was Scousers and I wanted to take them on but it wasn't happening. I saw a few of our but things felt different and I couldn't figure out why.

The Scousers were in the Scoreboard End, while I ended up in the United Road. Everything seemed weird. I was as streetwise as anyone and could always read a crowd, but now the clothes, the sounds, the mood and the signals were all different. Still, I figured there was bound to be fighting outside and I was having it.

They kept the Scousers in and I came out with Little Des from Salford. I kept saying, 'Right, we'll do this,' and all the time he was saying, 'No, no, it's changed.' I looked around for the firm, the lads, and couldn't see them.

'Right,' I said, 'let's go to United Road railway station, everyone will be there.'

'No, no, it's not happening,' said Des.

He stuck with me because he knew I had lost the plot and he was trying to look after me. I marched off to the station and stood on the platform with a few straight members. They would have let the Scousers out by now and escorted them to Warwick Road station. That meant they would be coming in soon.

The first train came in and it was packed with United.

'Right, the next train,' I said.

'No, the Scousers will be on it, you nutter,' said Dessie.

'Will they fuck,' I said.

As the next train came in, Des did not look happy, but he had to stick with me. The few straight members waiting on the platform were also moving away towards the steps; they knew they had missed the train they wanted and that the next one wouldn't be safe. Meanwhile I was in my own world.

'We are getting on this, we are going to town,' I insisted.

It pulled up and it was full, obviously, of Scousers. Fuck.

I opened the door, stepped on the train and smashed the nearest one in the head.

'Come on, you fucking Scouse cunts.'

I jumped back on the platform, followed by Des, and we had no choice but to leg up the stairs with a pack of them close behind, howling for my blood. We ran out of the station and I was thinking, fucking hell, things aren't how they used to be. This wasn't right. I can't have this going on, where is everyone?

'I'm not having this again,' I told Des. 'I'll soon sort this out.'

* * *

THE YOUNG LADS soon got to know who I was. It didn't take long. The likes of the Gallagher twins and Hotshot were only doing what I'd been doing when I was younger. Older lads like me would be plotting up while they'd be out running round, stirring it up. We called them the Young Uns.

As time went on I because the one lads looked to. I made sure that I was in charge, and eventually I took over completely. I wasn't having anyone telling me what to do. I was happy with that because I knew what I wanted to do. Other people would always chip in opinions, or often it would just go mental because you can't control a raging, pissed-up mob. But nine out of ten times I was off leading the way and then everyone was off with me. Most were quite happy to leave decisions to me and carry on having a beer. Of course I had missed several years and one or two others who weren't brought up in the Seventies were trying to make a name and influence things. That was fine by me. Sometimes things went wrong, but that wasn't a problem either. Ask Napoleon.

We never had gang names. Some of the lads occasionally referred to themselves as the Inter City Jibbers but that was a humorous label as much as anything. We could never have sat down like some of these mobs and invented a ludicrous name for ourselves. The Headhunters. The Bushwhackers. What sort of world are these people living in? Who sits there and says, 'We're the Baby Squad.' The Soul Crew, fuck me, there's no Soul Crew because they ain't got rhythm. It's childish. Any firm that invents a name for itself wants recognition that it hasn't earned by its exploits. We never needed to seek recognition. We were at it for thirty years yet this is the first book by a Man United hooligan. None of the lads would write it because they were too busy doing it.

Why do these other mobs beat people up and leave them with calling cards? That is juvenile thinking. What kind of brain is that? A person left with a card on him, kicked unconscious by a group of jackals. That was their mentality.

* * *

I WAS MARRIED within twelve months of coming out of jail, to Debbie. The poor girl did not have a clue about my past. I didn't keep it secret but I didn't advertise it. I wasn't normal, but what is normal? I got a bug when I was a kid and the bug was still in me and I didn't change one iota.

Our first wedding anniversary was derby day and I promised Debbie I would be home for 7pm. We'd had a big discussion and I'd accepted her deadline. This was a major break point in my life – do I carry on with what I'm doing, or do I really listen and change? If I had missed the derby it would have been the start of the end for me at the football. My compromise, to keep the peace in the house, was that I would be home for seven. Looking back, there was no way in this world that if the lads were still running around two hours after the game, I was suddenly going to say, 'See you, I'm off,' but that was what I thought.

Of course, it was a normal derby day: fighting in the morning, fighting outside the ground, fighting inside the ground, then fighting in town, bar to bar, hunting City in big gangs. I ended up charging into Rose's Bar in the city centre after the shout went up that City were in there. We went piling down the road into the boozer and there they were, so we ran in and smashed them, throwing tables and chairs on them for good measure. I saw Sully, a City fan I knew, and stopped him from getting battered (and not for the first time) because he was one of the old school. I couldn't let him get filled in because it would have been a liberty.

This was my last excursion of the night but it was still 10.30pm before I rolled up at my front door with a mate in tow, drunk but trying to pretend I'm not, knocking on the door like a mouse. It opened and there was a woman with tears down her face, and I'm saying, 'You'll be all right, just get your dress on and we'll go to a club.' Me trying to stand up straight, with her slumped over the dressing table sobbing her heart out and I'm saying, 'I'm back, aren't I?' I got no joy so I walked back out, went to the pub across the road and ended up in a nightclub in Chorlton until 4.30am.

* * *

IN 1984 WE drew Juventus in the Cup Winners' Cup. I decided I was going on a mad one to Turin because I had been locked up for a long time and needed a good blowout. Fourteen of us acquired some credit cards and we were off, to drink and have a jolly. We met on the Friday, left at dinner-time and went down to Harwich, which was not the normal way to go. Then I decided we were going to Sweden, which was ridiculous. So we boarded the twenty-six-hour over-nighter. It is not easy to jib on this boat but eventually we all did, pushing and shoving a bit and blagging our way past the two ticket inspectors. You were supposed to have a cabin but it didn't matter during the day.

We robbed the duty free of just enough booze to keep us going. Then the beer was coming, then it started to get chaotic. We all went to the disco. No women were going to be mithering us in our state and everyone got bladdered. A few of the lads went for a mooch and liberated a bag of money from a cabin. We had got three or four straight members with us and – I don't thieve – I can't go sneaking in rooms – but the other lads had no such scruples.

The bag was given to one of the straight members but now we were under suspicion from the boat security. We were the only ones laid down on different decks outside the bars, drunk, so it didn't take Sherlock Holmes. We knew there'd be problems when we came to get off in the morning but our trump card was Tommy and his pal, who looked too straught to be with us. Sure enough, we all got pulled by police and Customs except Tommy and this lad. It was tremendous. The problem was, some still had credit cards which they tried to hide but the coppers stripped everyone. Two were slung back on the boat, handcuffed in the brig.

We drew thousands of pounds on the credit cards, then at 5.30 we got off the train to Denmark with all this free money. We got off at some mad town somewhere in Sweden, about halfway to where we were headed, and found a big restaurant-bar. Even back then it was over £5 a pint, so the credit card was getting smashed again. There was hardly anyone in there but we had got the British mentality of half-five, pub.

We were only staying for one round – until one or two birds came in. The person with the credit card decides we'll stay for another drink. The Swedish barman has already taken our card, so we know it will be right. Within two hours, the place was in uproar – there were women and lads dancing, beer being ordered by the tray, and the man with the credit card, no-one has ever had more fingers pointed at him than this person that night.

'Five beers. Put it on his bill.'

'Four more over here and put it on his bill.'

We came out at half past one in the morning. One person was carried with his feet being dragged to sign this credit card bill. He didn't even know the name on the card, let alone what to sign, yet the barman smiled and took it. Then we led a Swedish conga through the town square, running through another bar that was closing, sixty people doing a conga over the tables and out the back door.

We ended up at the train station on the platform in the dark, all laid down with our bags and a train came in at 5.30. We didn't care where it was going, we just got on, got a seat and fell asleep. At a certain stage the hector appeared and wanted his tickets. No one was interested, he was told to fuck off and everyone fell asleep. I awoke to find an Alsatian in my face and a posse of police officers on the train. Fun and games, lies and more lies, and the copper in charge was told we couldn't buy tickets because there was no inspector on the platform and now this man wanted to charge us a fortune and a penalty on top. In the end we opened the bag from the boat, counted out the right cash and squared it off.

We eventually made it to Turin via Paris, where we were chased from a hotel because it came on top with the credit card. We had to hide on a building site and sleep there until the morning. In restaurants we were all eating as fast as we could in case it came on top. One of us later met the American writer Bill Buford, who had been following some of United's lads around while researching his book *Among The Thugs*.

> Someone from another group appeared, showing me a map, with an inky blue line tracing its route to Turin. It began in Manchester, then continued through London, Stockholm, Hamburg, Frankfurt, Lyon, Marseilles and finally stopped here. A great adventure, not unlike, I reflected, the Grand Tour that young men had made in the eighteenth and nineteenth centuries, and it had cost them – all eleven of them – a total of seven pounds.
>
> Seven pounds, I exclaimed, understanding the principle. What went wrong? They assured me they would be in profit on the return.

That's the way it was done in those days: leave with fuck-all, have a ball and come back with a few quid.

I knew all about Turin from my previous visit. We found ourselves at the train station early in the morning, just like the old days, and bought big bottles of wine for seventy-five pence each. It was like vinegar, but after the first half bottle we were away. We settled in a small park opposite the station and as the morning rolled on, more and more came over. More bottles of wine were being necked and eventually the park was rock solid with singing, dancing Reds. The police had to close the streets.

Probably because of the wine, I don't remember getting to the ground. I think we walked for a while and then jumped on a tram. We were no longer with the main group because we had lost the plot. We ended up not going in United's end – we had no tickets anyway – but got in the main stand and we were off it, singing and chanting. United were winning and I think we had scored and were through, but the game wasn't over. We jumped up and down on the fence like lunatics. United fans were in the far corner and we could see things being launched in there all game and people getting smashed heads. It was out of order.

When Juventus equalised we were ill. We made our way to the left-hand corner, with the game still going on, and missiles started coming from behind the goal at us. The fence was saving us but we were still half-pissed and egging them on, not realising the danger. This was a bearpit, not a football ground.

The end of the game came. Drunk as I was, I knew enough not to walk straight out, and I restrained the others. Instead we made our way to the opposite end of the stand and got out there to avoid being ambushed. It was frightening outside. The Italians are cunts. You know lads are going to get stabbed and slashed. They kept the main United back and then a fair mob of our lads went on the march and went looking for it, but we couldn't locate them because we had come out with the Italians. We were later told they marched into town, took on some Italians and gave it to them, then they took it to them again at the station. They all kept together and did well, had a good fight and they were happy with it.

My advice is never go to Turin and wander around the night before or after the game. Go together and stay together, because every person on a scooter is a potential lookout for the rest of them. It is one dangerous city – as are all the major Italian cities. It still goes on today and can be worse. You've got to be on your toes.

* * *

AS SOMEONE WHO was listened to in the firm, my life became a constant 'What are we doing?' 'Where are we going?' 'What next?' It was constant pressure, and sometimes you made wrong decisions. A midweek League Cup at Tottenham in March 1985 was one of my biggest rucks. Because it was a Wednesday night there were fewer of us than usual from Manchester, but we were bolstered by the Cockneys. One hundred and fifty of us, a small mob by our standards, made our way across the cross-roads after the game and it went off. The scuffles made us the focal point and Yids started coming from hundreds of yards away. Within about fifty yards our numbers had dropped to forty: the rest simply fucked off into the night. The scuffling hadn't yet got heavy but they had seen what was coming and they didn't fancy it.

I was with some young lads from Manchester, Robert from Peckham and his brother, and a few others. We got further up the road and Spurs were in front, at the side and behind. You couldn't go anywhere. They were sniping from every angle and though we were fighting them off, I thought I was going to die.

It got to a point where we could go no further and I told the group to stop. We halted and got our backs against the wall, so they couldn't surround us. They came from all sides. Coppers tried to hold off little groups of them but most got through and steamed in. Forty of us fought them in a space about fifteen feet wide. A couple of our young lads were cowering behind me and grabbed the back of my coat in terror. As the Spurs came in from each side, these two idiots were swinging me round like a shield. I punched and punched until my arms felt like lead but I could not move into space because these two were holding me and yelling with fear:

'O'Neill! O'Neill!'

I lost count of the number of punches I took, proper blockbusters. A mad Yid would fly in, lashing three or four blows, then another would come in from the side. My head began to swim but I kept going, my arms working like a threshing machine. Through sheer fear, the two kids behind me ripped my coat from collar to my waist. The coppers were little help and I'm sure some of them were arresting people just so they could fuck off out of there.

We had to carry on. With a bit of police help we finally managed to break away in the dark and headed further up the road. I led us right down a side street to get off the main road – and we ran straight into a group of black lads. We were just trying to escape the mayhem but we walked into the fire. They piled into us and we had to run back to the main road. It got worse and worse.

We eventually reached Tottenham Hale station, battered and bruised but still together. We knew we were never going to make Seven Sisters: we would die. We could see the entrance to the tube station and the promise of sanctuary, but a copper on a horse, in his sick wisdom, decided to block the entrance so we couldn't get in. We were still getting it from the Spurs because there were only three other coppers escorting us and they couldn't hold the mob back. Someone literally dived under the cop horse, through its legs and into the station, and we were so desperate to get off that road that the rest of us followed suit, running at the entrance two and three at a time and diving under the horse's belly. I will never know what that copper's game was but we had the incentive of all the thugs on us.

We survived with just a few minor wounds. We stayed on the platform as long as we could and eventually got a train and ended up in the Kings Cross/St Pancras area, a long time after the end of the match. There used to be a 12.30am train back to Manchester which we aimed for. We thought our ordeal was over and were at the back of the fire station at Euston and the Spurs were only there as well, charging out of the side street with poles, still at us. They knew that sooner or later we'd be turning up at Euston. We tried to hold them off but in the end had to fuck off into the train station, where more police were waiting. What a night. So for those who say United claim never to have been done, I can vouch that it came on top many a time. But so what?

CHAPTER TWELVE

THE I.C.F.

BIG, ORGANISED MOBS. That's what the early Eighties were all about, and we were the biggest of all. Man United were the only team to go away, game after game, and have the lads there. There might be a couple of hundred or there might be more but they would be there and were the only ones to go week in, week out, away from home. Even the police say that. A big mob sometimes hindered your intentions because you couldn't always get to the trouble and it brought the police in. So some would often split off and stay in the pub to avoid hassle. That was up to them. The thing with United was, everyone was coming from everywhere, and you didn't fuck people off because we were a family. We weren't elitist in that sense.

Others were. More than any other football gang, the West Ham Inter City Firm (those silly names again) cultivated their reputation. They were aloof, untouchable. They could destroy enemies without throwing a punch; lesser mobs would crumble and run rather than face these seemingly invincible East End hard men. Well, that reputation never cut any ice with us. We had grown up amid the worst football violence this country had ever seen. We were born to it. For all their arrogance and bravado, we knew they often hid behind weapons. To me that was a sign they were not as confident as they pretended.

In January 1983, while I was in prison, West Ham had brought what some people say was the best firm any English club ever brought to Old Trafford, for an FA Cup tie. They came early on the train, 3–400 strong and Cass Pennant and about thirty others went into the back of the United Road Paddock with ten minutes to go, and had a bit of a scuffle before they were chased out. This has since become part of their invincible legend, but like much of what they claim it doesn't stand up to scrutiny. Firstly, the main lads by this period all sat in the A, B and C Stands and in K Stand, above the away support. What was the point of going in the United Road when the boys weren't there? Secondly, where were they after the game? Gone, as usual. Leave early, have a little flurry and then fuck off before the main United firms come out and smash them to pieces. Those were their tactics, and they know it.

Chelsea claim to have once done something similar. They say that 250 of them left the Scoreboard End – where they endured cups of piss thrown down on them all game from the stand above – walked into the back of the Stretford End and allegedly 'took' it. In the words of Steve 'Hicky' Hickmott in his book *Armed For The Match*, 'the whole end scattered away from our primeval chant' and United were 'put to flight by the appliance of Chelsea science'. Hicky, you should donate all your criminal compensation to the United Old Boys' Association for that bullshit. I want to see you in the Dog's Bollocks pub in Thailand and I want free beer all day while I listen to your full account, and you'd better have witnesses to back it up, because I can't find any. If there's any glimmer of truth in this fantasy, tell me this: why when you left the Scoreboard did you not just take the staircase that led up to K Stand, where your piss-throwing tormentors were? That's where all our firm would have been. Well, you know why you never tried to get up there: it would have been the end of your precious Chelsea reputation.

The I.C.F. were the same. Once again they had failed to do

what we'd have done: get into the city centre for opening time, camp out in a couple of boozers and take on all attackers. They knew we would be there, ready and waiting, so what did they do, time and again? Come in at Piccadilly, pose a bit around the forecourt, few scuffles, big police presence, escort straight out of the city centre towards the ground.

Four days after our game in Turin, we played West Ham at home. I'd brought some CS gas, a novelty at the time, and still had it in my coat pocket. We expected them to show on the train again, and London Road and the Piccadilly Station approach, top to bottom, was full of United. Everyone had been in the pubs, cafes and amusement arcades from 10.30 that morning. I for one was desperate for a crack at them.

We got word that the train had pulled in and that 150 of them had got off, led by Bill Gardner. A few police stood guard outside the station but most were inside to manage the visitors. We couldn't wait, and charged up the approach, with me right at the front. The station doors swung open and a couple of coppers came out first, one with a dog. Next thing, the dog was on my back; I hadn't realised the copper had an extension lead and he set Wonderdog on me. This fucking wolf was well up for it. He ripped off my shirt and started chewing my back, and then the cops jumped on me. At the same time their colleagues forced the rest of the United back down the approach.

Even as I struggled I could see West Ham being let out. They never at any time tried to move away and look for trouble. Gardner was at the front, the big lump. They stood with the police around them with vans, clearing the way for them. At one point, halfway down, they all stopped to keep together and see what was in front of them. This mob was going nowhere except with police protection.

This was how the American writer Bill Buford described the scene in his book *Among The Thugs*:

They had walked down in three columns. Once they reached the High Street, they stopped, still in formation. At the front was a big, broad-shouldered man, about thirty-five. This was Bill Gardner. He stood there, feet planted apart, crossed his arms and waited. Next to him were his lieutenants, who had crossed their arms, their feet already apart, and waited. They were all dressed in the same manner: jeans, open leather jackets, T-shirts. Many had the same scar on their faces: the serrated hook across the cheeks, a knifing scar . . . They stood there until the police had cleared away all the United supporters.

I missed that little cameo as I was dragged off and slung in the back of a van. I tried to hide the can of CS under the seat but must have depressed the lid, because my eyes, face and throat started burning. When I jumped out of the van at Bootle Street police station I was kicking off about my back, the dog and my eyes, and they had to cart me off to hospital. After a check-up they bunged me back in the cells at Bootle Street.

I was woken up by the policeman who arrested me, now playing the Good Cop role. 'What's this?' he said pleasantly, producing the CS gas canister. 'It must be yours.'

It was now 5pm, and I had been arrested at about 11.30. They hadn't mentioned it before, so maybe they had only just found it, and couldn't prove it was mine.

'I haven't got a clue what you are on about.'

'It is a firearms offence to be in possession of this,' he said, still dead nice, thinking I was going to cough. No chance.

At 6pm I was charged and let out. Derek Whittaker was outside waiting and we went to the pub. I later denied threatening behaviour and what I found amazing was that the copper who arrested me forgot to mention his dog in his evidence. After a bit of legal argy-bargy, they agreed to bind me over for twelve months to keep the peace.

* * *

IN 1985, WE played West Ham in the quarter-finals of the FA Cup. The I.C.F. were accompanied on this trip by a cameraman and it would later feature in the documentary *Hooligan*. For once there was an indisputable record that shows up their 'invincible' bullshit.

Everyone was out once again for this one. I got into town just after 11am and crowds had already formed around Piccadilly Gardens. Suddenly it went off somewhere and United were charging about like lunatics. I found myself outside Woolworths chasing some West Ham lads. We saw Jeff Lewis in a bus shelter being arrested because he had twatted someone, so we all went over. We crowded round and insisted Jeff had been attacked and the copper let him go because he was so scared.

Then someone else was punched in Piccadilly Gardens and a copper grabbed a West Ham fan. Some of our mob wanted to beat up both the copper and the Cockney but I stopped them. Then little Mally Russell, who can't fight to save his life, and I were off chasing some more behind the back of Yates's Wine Lodge. I lost sight of this guy I was after but then clocked him sneaking back. I walked up and smacked him and he ran off again. I ended up chasing some more through Stephenson Square, with a mob of United behind me, and these West Ham were not stopping. I couldn't catch up so I stopped. Then, whack. I got twatted by this United fan who thought they'd been chasing me. I went ballistic.

'Oh sorry, sorry,' he pleaded.

These things happen. Then I was off back into Piccadilly. We still had not found their main mob, but stories were going round that they had come in very early and got through when hardly anyone was about. The groups we had scattered had all come in on the following train.

'Right,' I said, 'everyone is here. Let's think where they might be and let's go and find them.'

We knew they weren't in town or they'd have been spotted by now, so the march was on. We found out that the I.C.F. were in the Bull's Head on Chester Road, towards the ground. Typical – miles away from the action. We came out of town under the Mancunian Way and marched through some housing estate, hundreds of us, all the firm. We came to a park, then a side street, and the Bull's Head was in view. Police were stationed down the street but there were none with us. We charged down the side street and through the uniformed officers. Some West Ham standing on the corner fucked off back to the pub as quickly as they could. We got nearer and more police were waiting in lines with their batons out. West Ham were safely behind them and didn't come out of the pub.

Eventually they were escorted out and marched down the road. We were still trying to get at them and cut through a back street to a junction with another pub, the Northumberland. We were swarming out of this housing estate and over wasteland. Bill Gardner had come across the road to stand on the corner of the Northumberland with four blokes out of his mob as we emerged from behind the estate. It was a good pose, and no doubt he thought the police would pull him back over – until he realised the cops had left him and it was on top, with a few of our lads going directly for him. Bill soon saw the error of his position and retreated back to the protection of his firm.

We hassled them all the way to the ground, as the video they made will attest. Unfortunately we had endless hassle ourselves off their police escort and could not get through them, which is a shame. This was a big game for West Ham, an FA Cup quarter-final, and when we reached Old Trafford, trainloads of them were being marched up from Warwick Road. They now had a big mob together and I'll give them some credit, they made a push outside the ground and there were scuffles all over the place.

What I can't understand is that here they were, with this massive following in the Scoreboard, yet with ten minutes to go Bill Gardner stood up in J Stand and signalled for his firm to leave. Why didn't they wait to the end of the game and take it to United full on? Because they knew what was going to happen, that's why: United would take it to them, Scoreboard End, both sides, attack. In that scenario, Bill Gardner is not in charge, he's in danger of getting a dig because he's a face. So they come out of the ground early and who is in front of them? Nobody. Lads were scrambling to catch up to them. Where were they going? They were fucking off to the railway station, to leave the rest of the West Ham behind. Their priority was to get out as a mob and get to Piccadilly safe. If not, who were they going to fight?

As it happened, enough United did get out to attack them on the corner of Chester Road. You can see it on the documentary. What you don't see, and what you'll never hear off them, is Harry the Dog coming face to face with Bill Gardner. They knew each other, as they'd met in a bar in Bilbao during the 1982 World Cup. As it went tits up all around him, Gardner shouted to Harry, 'Whooah, we've had enough. Get them off us.' Let's see if they put that in any of their books.

I remembered back to when I was a kid and saw that big group of Scousers heading into town and realised what the game was – you have only won if you get back to Piccadilly in one piece. Well, any firm can do that if they leave ten minutes before the end. Not that they were there yet. The departing I.C.F. had a little victory as certain individual United mobs tried to catch up with them at different railway stations. When their train pulled in at Deansgate some United went at them. Gardner and his boys were off swinging punches and although the United there had a go they were obliged to back away. So West Ham had their little result, but only because they were staying ahead of the pack all the way. By the time they got to Oxford Road, they were staying on the train because there were hundreds of United fans there. They got back to Piccadilly and fucked off with their cameraman.

* * *

A YEAR LATER, it was our turn to visit them in the FA Cup. The match was due to be played on a Saturday but because of awful weather was twice rearranged at short notice. Three days on the trot I was at Piccadilly at twelve o'clock, waiting for the weather forecast, and it was bloody freezing. Finally by the Wednesday the weather had subsided but because of the disruption it was obviously a much smaller United contingent than normal that set off that afternoon to Upton Park. Our train was late arriving at Euston, so we didn't hang about and were straight on the tube. There were probably about 300 Reds in total and though we had a nice big group of lads, including the Cockneys, there were also loads of normal fans with us.

We pulled into Plaistow station in East London and for some reason a couple of lads said, 'Let's get off here.' This often happened on London trips – people stepping on and off tube trains, arguing about the best place to get off – but we had no plan to alight here and because we were running late for the game, most of us couldn't see the point.

'Get off.'

'No, stay on, where the fuck are you going?'

Now it may be that one of the Cockney Reds wanted everyone off because he knew West Ham drank around there. I don't know. All I can say is that myself and the rest of the lads knew fuck all about it. We wanted to get to the ground. But this big debate led to more and more piling off and the next thing I knew everyone was leaving, including all the straight goers, who understandably didn't want to lose the safety of being with the mob.

I was not too happy because it was a rushed decision with nothing planned, but once they were all moving there was no point arguing. Certainly no-one walked up those stairs expecting a fight. If we had, I would not have been sauntering along in the middle of the crowd, queuing up to get on the escalator. I'd have been at the front preparing the lads and getting ready to storm out and smash all comers.

I was only halfway up the escalator when the first people went through the ticket turnstiles. The next thing I heard a big roar. It had obviously gone off. West Ham were waiting across the road in the dark and tooled up to their eyeballs. Those first few to go out were hit by everything.

The reason I am setting the scene is because of the self-serving account of this in Cass Pennant's book *Congratulations You Have Just Met the I.C.F.*, not by Cass but by some of their lads who were there. They claim they had been tipped off by a Cockney Red that we were getting off at Plaistow to take one of their main pubs, the Brit, and so they waited to ambush us in two other pubs next to the station, the Raglan and the Vic. When they saw the first twenty Mancs come out of the station they steamed in to force them back inside, as they knew if we all got out they'd be fucked. They also claim in their account that 'both sides were tooled up'. Well I know *they* were – they had ammonia, pickaxes, hammers, bottles, shovels, axes and knives. Someone in a builders' van was even doling weapons out to them.

To put the record straight about this, when have we ever gone tooled up? We were brought up on fighting. No hammers, no bats. Secondly, at least half of our group were straight members and non-combatants. Thirdly, if it was planned, would we really have been so stupid as to have allowed them to pin us in the tube station? Would we have been nonchalantly heading up the escalator, oblivious to the chance of an ambush? And fourthly, we'd come on the train, right through Euston, lines of police, cops on the train. What weapons were we supposed to be carrying? Nail files?

We found out later a sixteen-year-old United lad was caught outside in that first rush and was stabbed with a kitchen knife in the chest, puncturing his lung. As he lay on the floor bleeding, they came back and booted him until a British Transport copper saved his life. The word on the night was that he was dead; later on it was that he was alive but critical. Another young lad needed eleven stitches when he was stabbed in the cheek.

We couldn't see what was going on because it was so dark and people were pushing on the escalator to get up. I fought my way to the top, jumped the turnstile and got into the concourse. I was quickly told that a small number of United had walked out and had immediately been attacked with weaponry. They had either legged off down the road or run back inside the station. No-one knew what was going on.

Next thing, some of us were in the concourse with these two big doors open and stuff flying in. I bawled at everyone to get over and they started to come.

'Over here, all fucking get here now.'

There was no fighting, in fact I couldn't even see a West Ham fan, but bricks and bars were coming through the two big doors. People panicking, it was so dark and noisy and there was a lorryload of metal coming through at us, so we closed the doors to get organised and stop this stuff hitting everyone. We were accompanied by four British Rail coppers who were inside absolutely shitting themselves, but at least had the presence of mind to bolt the big doors. We could hear West Ham outside kicking them.

I was now at the front and got everyone together. To our right was another small double door, so my brother and I went and opened one half of it; the other half was bolted. I grabbed a broken stool that I think had come from a fruit and veg stall and waited for West Ham to rush the door. Our kid jammed his foot against the bottom of it, leaving a gap just big enough for one person, and I stood there smashing them with half a stool as they tried to get through. The coppers yelled at us to shut the door but our kid and I were loving it. We didn't panic and we kept it together, as much for the straight members there as for ourselves.

Each time I smashed them, they'd move back. We would shut the door, then open it again to get a few more shots in. After the third time, I said, 'Right, we're going out.' Not everyone wanted to, but someone had to take charge. We got ready to open the small door. Things outside seemed to have calmed a bit but it was still very spooky.

We got everyone together, got through the doors and as we got out, missiles flew at us again. They were actually fighting, for the first time. They surged into us but there was not much hard contact; it was like fighting phantoms or shadows in the dark. It was so dark and confusing we could not see what weapons they had or how many of them there were – there could have been twenty or there could have been 200, I couldn't say. All I could see was the group near me when I got out, and they all had weapons. One was squirting ammonia from a white container.

In the end they forced us back in but didn't follow – they certainly didn't fancy coming in after us, even with all their weapons – so we bolted the door again. Then came the classic. Through a gap in the door I saw a big West Ham fan brandishing a traffic bollard. It was over his head and he was charging at the door. I grabbed my trusty half-stool again, and as he came to launch his bollard at the door, our kid opened it fully and this bloke's momentum brought him flying through. Then I was on him, whacking him with the stool. He scrambled on his hands and knees. Our kid whacked his pal, then everyone surged to get him. He scrambled out the door, the big lump, and the only thing that got him out was fear.

We got away from Plaistow in the end because whoever was out there eventually fucked off. It can only last so long. It was proper scary for some people but I was on it and was buzzing all the way to the ground. People were also talking about the kid who'd got stabbed. We went in the seats, next to the United fans behind the goal, and not once did they have a go at us until the end of the game. Some United even ran on the pitch when we scored. I also saw the big, bollard-wielding Hammer I'd creamed with the stool; he was walking around the pitch with a cut head where I'd whacked him. He must have wanted everyone to see it and asked for first aid. Towards the end his mates tried it on in the seats, but Grogan and Co. were up and at them and fucked them off.

The game had been a draw and so we played them at our place the following Sunday. You can imagine what was waiting for them. Guess what? They didn't even sell out their ticket allocation. Did the I.C.F. show? I won't even bother answering.

* * *

ONE INFAMOUS CLASH with West Ham drew more headlines than all the others combined. It was on a cross-Channel ferry on August 7, 1986. United were playing a pre-season game against Ajax in Amsterdam, while West Ham were also playing in Holland. About twenty of them found themselves on the same ferry as 150 Reds and a fight started. West Ham occupied a bar at the top of the ferry and defended their high ground. The fight became so notorious because it lasted well over an hour, because the captain turned the ferry back to Harwich, because it destroyed the chances of getting English clubs back in Europe after the ban imposed for the Heysel Disaster, and because some of those involved later got very long prison sentences. A prosecutor later described it as 'tantamount to an act of piracy on the high seas', which was overdoing things a bit.

I wasn't there, so the only reason I mention it here is to correct another West Ham myth, or rather a couple of myths: one, that it was a major 'victory' for them over their hated rivals from Manchester, and two, they wrote in a book, 'We counted twenty-two stretchers going off with drips and some Mancs even leaving the boat in wheelchairs.'

On the first point, the majority of United fans there were barmies – not hardcore hooligans but football fans out for a drink and a good time who would pile into a fight if they were drunk or giddy enough. This was not out firm, by any stretch of the imagination. And on the second point, let's put it this way: you lying, spinning Cockney bastards. We accept you had a result but to write that twenty people were taken off in stretchers and wheelchairs, you are an embarrassment to being a football hoolie and a chap.

Little Dessie was one of those on the boat, travelling with a group of mates to enjoy the delights of Holland in the summer.

The barmies were downstairs singing and getting tanked up. It was happy days for them. West Ham were quiet. The only chance was for them to defend an enclosed space and they went up to this bar at the top of the boat. When it first kicked off, me and a few others weren't drunk and tried to stop it. It was pointless having a fight on that ferry. 'Fuck this,' we said, 'we'll see them on the other side, leave it till then.' But they weren't having it.

The West Ham were a good firm, no doubt about that, and it was a class fight. In the end, when the barmies realised they couldn't do it on their own, we were up those stairs on level pegging. I was at the front with a hosepipe and there were pots bouncing off my head. Someone turned the hose on but we didn't realise it was connected to the sea and the pressure coming through was enormous. It lifted me off the ground like Mary Poppins.

They allegedly counted all these stretchers and wheel-chairs when the boat returned to Harwich. Absolute bollocks. Who were they for? They walked off in an orderly fashion back in the UK, but we stayed on and went back over for the football. West Ham didn't have to get off, they chose to. I can say hand on heart that not one of us walked off that boat with an injury. And the only people who got nicked were barmies for being barmy and full of keg. That is the Eighth Wonder of the World, seeing the barmies on the rampage.

The I.C.F. defended themselves and they did it well. They chose the high ground, and you can't fight going uphill. I have tried it many a time, and you can do it without injuries. So why put a silly spin on it?

Eventually the *Hooligan* documentary, the fight on the ferry, and the undercover police investigation called Operation Own Goal brought the I.C.F. to a halt. Some of their main faces apparently went into the rave scene in a big way, or into security. I will remember them as a very solid firm who could definitely have a fight but who, like the Scousers and Millwall, always backed themselves up with weapons because they were afraid of losing. Whereas getting done to me was part of the game – so long as we had a great time.

CHAPTER THIRTEEN

SCOUSERS

THE BITTER RIVALRY between Manchester and Merseyside has been well documented. For many fans from both sides, that rivalry was even more bitter off the pitch than on it. I was never quite sure why the Scousers resented us so much: perhaps it was because no matter how successful Liverpool in particular may have been – and let's face it, they were the business on the park for a good ten years or more – we were always perceived as being the bigger and more attractive club. And maybe they hated us so much off the pitch because we took it to them and challenged them on their own doorstep.

From our point of view, while I'm sure a lot of United fans were jealous of their bulging trophy cabinet and their antics around Europe, it was the activities of their more lowlife followers that really stirred the pot. I would like to see a record of the number of football fans who have been cut, slashed, or robbed by the Scousers; not just United fans but the likes of Ipswich, straight members, innocent parties. That's why we labelled them the vermin: not their ordinary fans but their snidey weasels who carried blades. They looked for victims. It was never like that in Manchester. Yes, you would see the odd story of a stabbing at a United game, but it was rare. Yes, in the wild days of the early Seventies people did get beat up or get a dig just for wearing colours, but it was like that everywhere. And when we went away and it came on top, we didn't just get a dig – we got leathered. That's what made us what we were; every time you went away we knew some loon was out there looking for you.

The only time I remember Scousers getting cut by United supporters was in revenge for one of our lads being carved up on a previous trip. We were playing Liverpool, and were walking down Scotland Road in the dark. The Scousers tried to come behind us from an embankment. We whipped back round and a couple of lads slashed two of them. That was the only time and it was specifically two lads that did it because they had reason. I have never known United fans to travel anywhere else with weapons.

We didn't want to slash people, and we didn't want to beat up straight members. We wanted the opposing mob. Our history shows it. So let's put the record straight, as the Scousers have very selective memories. We went on the Kop, the Kemlyn Road twice and the Main Stand at Goodison. Facts. We took it to them like no other firm ever did.

I ran a coach to Liverpool and led them into the Kemlyn Road with 100 other United. We got in a couple of minutes before kick-off and some of the Scousers down below were on it and tried to have a go in the passageway. The rest of us scrambled over the turnstiles in time and they fucked off upstairs. We carried on up, having it with a few of them on the way. By the time we got to the top, I was at the front and they all knew we'd arrived. The United section was to our right. We came into the gangway and I got a hot cup of tea straight in my face. There was nothing I could do because everyone behind me was pushing to get up. An arm swung at me but then the Scousers scrambled away because there was no stopping us.

The Scousers should have been waiting for us inside because they knew we had the tickets – they mixed with the ticket touts, who all deal with each other. As the police came in we jumped in all the empty seats they had vacated. Then the police got us. But at least we were there; what more could we do? They should have been there and had it.

About twenty-five minutes into the game we went down the back. Scousers knew the score and they came down for a look. 'Fuck off!'

Pie trays went, the lot. We cleared them out. We ended up back in the seats after staying down there through to half-time. Now we know the problem will be coming out, but there are only one or two coppers in the stand – underneath there were no coppers when it went off. We hold back for two minutes, then come down and we know it is going to happen. All the Scousers run screaming at us. We go straight out, some trying to have a go and we give it them and about three of the lads get nicked. Then we are forced round to the Anfield Road End.

Another incident you never hear the Scousers mention was when 200 United went on the Kop in the early Eighties. I was in jail at the time, but apparently the United end was full and this 200 were hanging around outside the game a good while before kick-off trying to find a way in. The chief copper, for some reason, took the mad decision to put them in the Kop before it filled up. They eventually found themselves shoved in the far right corner as you look at the pitch but they sang and wound up the Kop and the Kemlyn Road throughout the whole game. The Scousers went berserk trying to get through the police lines and at them but couldn't shift them. As far as I know no other team has ever taken a mob on the Kop and stayed there.

* * *

IN OCTOBER 1984, we played Everton away. I was fresh out of prison and full of piss and vinegar. I'd heard all the stories of life and death battles with the Scousers while I'd been inside, all the slashings and cowardly ambushes. Well not this time. We were going to do it properly.

Seven coaches arrived that morning outside the Dog and Partridge pub in Old Trafford. That's 350 top boys. We had managed to acquire 250 tickets for Everton's Main Stand through a spiv who got them from the club, and we were going in there to take it to them on their own turf. Everyone outwardly looked calm but inside I'm sure most of us were at fever pitch.

We got to Liverpool without picking up a police escort, came through Croxteth and pulled up. The lads piled off and we waited for everyone to get together before setting off on foot. Bystanders stared with mouths open as we went through back streets, cut through the back of some church and came out behind the Gwladys Street end. At the corner of the Gwladys Street and the Main Stand we twatted a few Everton, then bowled down towards the turnstiles. The road was now in uproar. Scousers were coming out of all the pubs near the ground but we were solid together.

Our idea was to get inside as quickly as possible before the cops could stop us. The first twenty-five or so got in but then the coppers blocked the turnstiles to stop the rest of us and pushed us along to a couple of other turnstiles. Those inside were on the stairs, battling back and forth and we could hear the noise. We also saw Scousers flying through other turnstiles further down to get there before us, so we now went mad trying to get in.

Eventually the coppers lost the plot and every one of us got in over the turnstiles. The minute each person got in he immediately ran upstairs to join the action. By the time I got over there was no action: there were too many United for them and Everton had retreated to the other side. As more Everton piled up the stairs, we were over and at them, fighting over the seats. Meanwhile scuffles were still going on downstairs. But they were never going to move us now. Eventually the coppers got in in sufficient numbers and it calmed down.

As the game kicked off we were all eyeballing each other and some of them are shouting, 'Yer gonna get cut after,' and all that Then the first goal went in. En masse, we jumped up and charged at them. Give them their due, they fought back. The second goal went in: same thing. Up and at them, more fighting, police break it up. Third goal; same again. The coppers couldn't quell it.

When the fourth one went in we stayed in our seats. Fuck it, we were knackered. That was the end of the fighting that day. We lost 5–0 and their police made sure we weren't causing them any more grief after the game. Despite the result it was a great day for us, while the Everton were visibly ill over the liberties we had taken.

The following year, we found ourselves drawn against Liverpool in the FA Cup semi-final. It was to be played at Goodison Park. By the mid-Eighties a good cup run was as exciting as it got for us on the pitch, so the hype was revved up to the max. Our plan was to catch the train from Victoria at around half ten. You would not believe the firm we had there. Like the Duke of Wellington said, I don't know what they did to the enemy but by God they frightened me. Every scarred old face had come out of the woodwork and all the new young mobs were there.

We knew Liverpool would be waiting for us in their city centre with everything they could muster. We also knew that Everton were playing in the other semi-final at Villa Park, and some would be boarding trains at Lime Street at about the time we would arrive. Two full firms of Mickeys to attack for the price of one: perfect. We knew it would be horrible, but we were ready. We crammed – and I mean crammed – into every available space on that train, like soldiers crowding onto a troop ship. And I reckon the atmosphere was probably not far off the Allied troops as they sailed over the Channel on D-Day, a mixture of trepidation, determination and pure, 100 per cent excitement.

There has been some confusion since about what happened next. Our train slowed down as it came through Edge Hill station on the outskirts of Liverpool city centre and then juddered to a halt in a tunnel a good mile and a half from Lime Street. Some people believed that the emergency cord was pulled and that was why we stopped in no man's land. But as we had passed through Edge Hill, I saw loads of cops, vans and empty buses waiting around the station. What were they doing there?

I believe that the Scouse cops that day planned to take us off at Edge Hill, to avoid the Everton at Lime Street. They would then escort us to the ground. This was something they had never done before and on the face of it was a bright move – only they had reckoned without the fact that the train was massively overcrowded and must have weighed far more than it should. I bet 800 Reds were on that train. For some reason the brakes either couldn't handle it or didn't work properly, with the result that we overshot the station and ended up in this tunnel.

So what did we do? We got off, and started marching to Lime Street. I kid you not, hundreds of United boys, jumping off in the pitch dark, negotiating live wires and the risk of trains coming the other way, set off to confront the Scousers. A Manchester copper was in the front carriage and tried to stop the first lot of lads. He was bricked and brushed aside. It was one of the maddest things I've ever seen. People were falling down manholes in the dark, tripping over sleepers, splashing through pools of oil, but at the same time we were loving it.

After about half a mile, some Liverpool coppers appeared over an embankment. They were going barmy.

'You mad bastards,' yelled one. 'You could have been killed.'

'All that's getting killed are them wankers who are in that station waiting for us,' came the response.

They turned the power off on the lines and managed to stop some of the lads but at least 400 kept going. The coppers were running around like loons, having kittens, but nothing was stopping us.

You can only imagine the scene that greeted the Evertonians waiting on their platform at Lime Street. Hundreds of Mancs, half of them blackened with soot and coal dust, emerging down the train tracks on foot, then breaking in to a trot as they sighted the enemy, and every single one of them chanting over and over again:

'War! War! War!'

We charged up a ramp and through Lime Street like a demented plague of locusts, laying waste. Some Everton ran off but then tried to come round the streets in a loop and get back at us but we fucked them off. Then we charged out of the station and down the road. There, outside St George's Hall, we saw the Scousers' full turnout: 700 of them, all craning their necks in our direction.

We didn't hesitate. With 'War! War!' still booming out, we flew straight across the road and at them – and they fled. Seven hundred mickeys in full, disorderly, panicking flight. Glorious. Then we stood firm on the crossroads, daring them to come back and do their worst. Some of them did mass together to have a go but we legged them again. No-one had ever done anything like that at Liverpool before, and no-one has done it since.

We set off to the ground in buoyant mood. The day was already a police nightmare: they had to look after the Everton going to Villa, the Scousers waiting for us in town and us marching to the ground. Then there was the other half of our firm, who had been forced back to Edge Hill. They were taken straight to Goodison and were held behind the Park End, bit they grew restless and, in tens and twenties, managed to escape the police cordon and regroup outside the Stanley pub.

Liverpool's mob, which we had seen off, had headed straight for the ground, no doubt hoping to start wasting United shirt-wearers and families in their usual merciless manner. They carefully avoided any further contact with us. What they weren't counting on, however, was the second half of the United firm; they had no way of knowing that several hundred more lads were at the ground already.

Their faces must have been a picture when they arrived in the vicinity of the stadium, only for another massive United mob to steam out of a side street next to the Stanley. United scattered them all over the dual carriageway. A few of them pulled out blades and one or two coats got slashed but they were had off again, scurrying away into the side streets and alleys.

The police were coming from everywhere now and eventually corralled United back towards the Park End; only when they were again cordoned off did the Scouse firms start to reappear. They looked shell-shocked. Quite a few went up to the United ranks and asked how the fuck this firm had got from Lime Street so quickly.

'We didn't,' was the reply. 'That's another firm. We got off at Edge Hill.'

The point was proved when the main mob turned up under escort. Stories were swapped about what had gone on. I was with my brother on Bullens Road and the street was half of them and half of us but no way were we letting them past. Just before kick-off they mobbed up to have a go. We were still outside the Bullens Road, with Grogan and Co. to the fore. They came off the dual carriageway and everyone turned and saw them off again.

The game was a 1–1 draw, which meant a replay at Maine Road in the middle of the following week. Outside it was the usual post-match war. Our mob now was enormous and little fights were breaking out on the edges all over the place. Some lads went to the car park to protect the straight members, because we knew they'd be getting attacked. The upshot was a great day for us, and a disaster for the Scousers.

The replay was an even more emphatic result. One of the lads wrote an account of the replay for *Red Issue*. It's an accurate version of events and more detailed than my memory allows:

Noon was the earliest time mooted to meet in town, with maybe eight pubs mentioned, all within a decent area so it wouldn't take much to pull everyone together. The feeling was the mickeys would show up mid to late afternoon at the earliest, so people drifted in without much urgency. As the afternoon wore on more and more faces turned up and a hefty mob developed, occupying a swathe of town, with fifty in this pub, a couple of hundred in the next. Lads took it upon themselves to go and check the various stations at irregular intervals and watch the services come in, without reward.

Given the lack of opposition, there was nothing to do but have a beer and the afternoon turned into a big drink. Maine Road held 50,000, so roughly 20,000 dirties were expected but as afternoon turned to evening there was still no sign of any of them.

'This is ridiculous, there's just none of them about at all.'

'I'll tell you what them mickeys are going to do, they're all going to dive on them specials. They're not even going to come on the service, we won't even see them.'

Word went round to meet at the Gamecock, a pub at the Moss Side end of Hulme. Some lads even walked there to kill time. The contrast to the non-stop action of the previous Saturday couldn't have been more pronounced. A constant trickle of reports came in from each of the stations. No sign of any of them. It was inconceivable that the Scousers would stay away, so it was surmised that Liverpool's alleged mob were indeed sneaking in amongst the civilians on the specials.

The first special was due in at 5:30pm. Logic indicated that the police would either escort them or, more likely, bus them to the ground. Without any concrete information, no major moves were made and yet again it turned into a drink, with small war parties and individual scouts constantly mooching off looking for the enemy.

The first solid info came in not long after the first special had arrived. Some lads had sighted a fleet of buses at the back of Victoria, presumably for transporting the bin-dippers to the ground. United had been drinking for over five hours now and weren't in the mood for walking back into town to tangle with an organised police operation. Even the most optimistic thug realised the best that could be hoped for was chucking bricks at buses. That had never been United's style. Everyone stayed at the Gamecock, figuring that we'd go to the ground and meet them there. A semi-final replay against Liverpool with not two hours to kick-off and we'd not had so much as a sniff of a Scouser.

It was decided to move to the ground, so perhaps 700 headed south to the hovel. Numbers swelled as various other small firms were collected from pubs and street corners. For a nobble, we made our way down Great Western Street, where coaches parked up in those days. Sure enough there were coaches full of Scousers. There wasn't a huge police presence, just a few dotted about. The bin-dippers were all singing, feeling secure on their buses, when we made our appearance. Suddenly everything went quiet; they knew what we were all about.

They were mostly ordinary fans, but a couple of coaches of Scouse barmies chose that moment to pull up. They got a bit silly, shouting abuse, thinking the police would save them if it came down to it. There weren't enough coppers there though. The look on their faces as we made our way through was a picture. It was a never-ending stream, it must have looked about half a mile long and ten yards wide. These barmies made the fatal mistake of giving it Munich and all that, and elements of the firm took offence and went for them. United were soon skittling them. A couple of the Scousers were quite handy as it goes, and they stuck it out quite gamely. They didn't understand the rules of this game though, and it wasn't long before they were getting ragged all over. The police came in on motorbikes, and they'd obviously called for reinforcements, so it was time to do one, leaving damaged Scousers lit by blue flashing lights. The column of hundreds instantly dissolved into tens and twenties and split up down the various side streets that make up Moss Side. Word was spread in those few seconds to meet at the Parkside, which was on the 'Scouse' side of Maine Road that night.

Not ten minutes later, the majority of the firm drifted up to the Parkside, hopeful of a real do. These hopes were dashed as it became apparent that the pub was full of United. Some teams had travelled via the Sherwood and the Claremont, but they were both securely Mancunian. Other pubs like the Osborne and the Lord Lion were similarly local. Where were all the Scousers? We heard their coaches were also being parked up at Hough End, ergo they'd be in the Princess. A medium-sized team drifted over in that direction but it was another non-starter; yet again they were just scarf wearers.

They went for a wander round the ground on their way back and came rushing back with news. The police were unloading the buses from Victoria at the back of the Kippax. Elements of Liverpool's firm were seen, mingling with the rest of the punters off the specials. As had been surmised, they'd bottled it. Finally, seven hours after the first lads had been in town, we had a solid contact.

There was some dissent as to the correct approach, but it was ended with these words: 'Forget the time and trying to go and do it near the death when the police are going, let's just go and do it now.'

Now, the area round Maine Road is good for splitting a firm up so it appears only a fraction of its size until you bring it together at the point of tactical interest. In this case, we rejoined behind the Platt Lane end occupied by the Scousers. The ground was segregated along the halfway line, with United having the North Stand. It was thick with Scousers queuing up to get in, but they were happy to back off. They weren't the target, though a few got a dig as we went through and things got said. This was discouraged by the majority though, as we didn't want to bring it on top with the police till we'd got to grips with their lads. As it happens, the police did get a whiff of it, but amazingly, they were happy to contain the scene of trouble rather than sort it all out.

There's a lane that runs the full length behind the ground at the back of the terraced streets and empties out on the Kippax car park. The firm vanished down there with their intentions clear: up to the end and a straight charge into them as quick as possible. Alleyways run off on the houses' side. We'd passed two or three of these ginnels when out of passage number four saunter seventy or so Scousers. A shout went up from the vanguard of our firm. It was dark and they probably reacted to the noise before they had a proper look at what they were facing but fair play to them, they stood. Numbers can't be made to count over a narrow frontage, and that alleyway holds seven or eight wide at best. The Scousers had emerged a mere ten yards or so ahead of the front line and it was roar up and in on both sides.

They were game but in their position they had little

choice. It was definitely do or die, outnumbered ten to one as they were, and a brutal toe-to-toe slugfest developed. They were slowly forced back by the weight of numbers. Game as they were, the Scousers were slowly back-pedalling and the opening to the Kippax car park was getting closer. I don't know if it was the realisation of the numbers they faced, or if their bottle simply went. They weren't entirely stupid, they knew what would happen to them in the wide open space of the car park. You could tell that the heart had gone out of them, because even though we were still having it with their frontline, you could see the press of bodies behind them slackening as the back few got off to save themselves.

Then events reached that critical point where the last fifteen or twenty who stuck it out were overwhelmed. Things rapidly got out of hand as the Scousers were battered and booted all over. One of them managed to pick himself up, quite a big bloke. He'd just got himself straightened up when a kid from Cheetham Hill ran in. I don't know where he got it from but I can still see the Woodpecker cider label on the bottle. Bang right over his head. Unsurprisingly the bloke dropped like a sack of spuds.

I don't want to sound like a peace negotiator here, but I'd been toe to toe with these Scousers for thirty yards down this alley. We'd gained a little bit of respect for them. Now Scousers being Scousers, that last fifteen had to be put down. No question. Once they were down, enough was enough. Some lads at the back of our firm were making a proper meal out of it though. These Scousers were still getting battered, mainly by lads who had neither the will nor the aptitude to have been in the front line a few minutes earlier. One mickey had been bottled; things were generally going too far. So I found myself saying to some of our own lads, 'Look, enough's enough. Leave it now, they're done in. They're finished.'

Some saw their arse at this. 'What do you think would happen to us if twenty of us were down in Liverpool? Do you think that any of them would try and save you? This is our chance to do these bastards some damage for all the straight goers over the years.'

If they were peeved, I was gutted. I could hear mayhem going on behind the Kippax, and there I was protecting scouse casualties from lads who should have had the same mayhem as their first priority. Some lads justified it saying that if they hadn't been Scousers, they'd have left them.

The police finally made an appearance, with ambulances close behind. Exit stage left and down to the Kippax to catch up with events. Picture a scene of total carnage. The whole of the car park was in uproar with police horses charging about.

United had chased Liverpool and backed them off across the car park into the other half of the Kippax, full of United. They weren't the firm, but with plenty of game barmies and handy lads stood around, put a few hundred mickeys in front of them and they soon knew what to do. Liverpool had gone from a reasonably tight defensive situation to being surrounded and cut to pieces in a few seconds. It all spilled over into the streets and alleys surrounding the ground. Mickeys were getting pinned down, picked off and split up. You got to the stage of wondering who was who. You'd find yourself in a small island of calm and the next minute you'd realise the lads walking parallel were scouse and off it would go again. And again, and again. Some scouse teams made attempts to regain the car park and had a token go, only to get blitzed. The half hour preceding kick off was non-stop mayhem. The police finally regained some order with a little ultraviolence of their own as the numbers thinned.

We were walking back to the Kippax thirty-strong when twenty lads came out of a side street. They looked the part, but none of us knew them. We walked across the road towards them and when we came within five yards or so they stepped back with that stance. Obviously they were Liverpool. One of us said, 'Right, this'll be the best one of the day.' Some of the lads I was with were amongst those who'd been at the front in the alley, but this would be even better. Fair play, they stood initially and traded blows, but then they made the mistake of legging it up one of the terraced streets instead of back towards the stadium. We chased them but they were hard to catch; it must be something in the genes. The back half dozen or so got tripped up and anyone who's been in that unfortunate situation couldn't help feeling for them. Still, they were game and they were Scousers, so they got a bit of a kicking. Their mates stood at the top of the road, shouting for us to leave them but they refused all invitations to come and rescue them.

An old boy in a vest opened his front door and went, 'What's going on here then?'

'It's just a few Scousers who've pushed their luck and now it's all gone wrong on them.'

'Oh, well there's nothing wrong with that, I just thought it was the other way round and those were United fans getting bashed around. I'm a Red me, I'll leave you to it.'

With that, he shut his front door.

Into the match then, and I happened to be right near the segregation in the main stand. We went behind to a Paul McGrath own goal and were all gutted at half-time. I'd had nothing but beer all day, so I walked back to the seats with a pie in one hand and a pint in the other (oh remember the days). The segregation was merely a couple of lines of tape with stewards sat down the middle. I'd not even reached my seat when Bryan Robson was sent on a run. The next minute I watched a twenty-five-yarder fly into the top corner. Our half erupted. One scouser with me jumped up and came out with Munich so I tossed my pint in his face and followed it up with a meat and potato. Pathetic really, but I did it. Verbals followed and a few of us went on a charge. The police were having none of it, and it all calmed down. We retook our seats in much better mood. With perhaps ten minutes left Sparky made it 2–1. Our half of the ground exploded. Yet again we're doing them in a semi. It helped to make up for the Milk Cup in 83. At the final whistle the contrast couldn't have been greater. The Scousers were slinking off into the night whilst we dived on the pitch en masse for an impromptu celebration. Robson was carried off on the shoulders of the crowd; it was a glorious United moment.

It was inevitable that someone would suggest a wander towards the Platt Lane end where a fair few Scousers were stood on the seats giving it the big come on behind the protection of a fifteen foot fence. They were clambering up as if to come over it, so we all stepped back to say come on down here and we'll have it.

What a lad he must have been; only one of them did it. Typical scouse: hundreds of them threatened to come over the top, one did, and I'm in two minds as to whether he just fell off. He hit the deck beside the advertising hoardings and he may as well have been thrown into the wolf pit. I'm sure the lads nearest him drew straws as to who'd leather him. We made a determined effort to get over the fence and they backed up the stand but the police were straight in and had it split up before it had really begun. The coppers moved us back up the pitch, so the word was Rusholme High Street, fifteen minutes.

Outside it seemed that the majority of the Scousers did a cover-up job and vanished into the night. Compare and contrast our performance in their city the previous weekend. All the Scousers left in Manchester were at or heading for Victoria, so by bus, cab and foot, United followed. Half an hour later we were plotted up near the Arndale. The mob was huge, upwards of 900 lads across a dozen bars. The usual scouting parties had gone off to the station and it didn't take them long to report back. The buses were coming in at the back on the north side of the station where the Arena is now. The police were bringing the buses in by the half dozen and trying to keep it all moving, but with the traffic it was a slow process. They didn't have enough buses to do the job in one go, so once they'd unloaded it was back to Maine Road to do it all again.

Once we'd got a feel for the timing of it all, the mob moved as one up to the Ducie Bridge pub opposite the back of Victoria. Sure enough six buses full of mickeys appeared in no time. One look and we charged straight at them. God knows what we thought we were going to do, they were on buses after all. I suppose we just wanted to stop them in the traffic and get it on. The looks on their faces as we surrounded them changed from abuse to sheer horror. They didn't want to get off and have a go, so the buses got clunked quite severely, followed by a window or two going through. Just as it looked bleak for those on board, the traffic freed up a little and they moved off again.

In no time we were at the back of the station opposite the penned-in Liverpool fans. We made a charge straight for them. The police had it all sorted and repelled us straight away. Liverpool tried to make it look good and made a token charge that had no chance of breaking through. It merely served to rev up the atmosphere. In a move I still don't believe to this day, the coppers chose that moment to toss the Scousers off the buses, outside the cordon. Big mistake. We charged them and some made the mistake of standing. They got leathered; there was chaos as the mickeys scrambled to get back on the buses.

The dibble intervened and pushed United back past the Ducie Bridge and up the main road. Having the police in front of us was easily sorted though. About turn and head back round to the front of the station, the police now in pursuit. Picture it. Nigh on 1,000 lads charging through the front of Victoria trying to get to the platforms hosting the specials. We were giving it, 'War! War! War!' and the acoustics of the old station roof made it sound awesome. It proper thundered round. The police chasing us caught up though, and more who hadn't came flying in from in front of us and pushed us out of the Victoria.

We made another charge to get round the back, but fate chose that moment for a few more buses to turn up from Maine Road. Unbelievably, 100-odd got off the buses and charged. What they were thinking I don't know. Some of them looked like their lads, but others just looked like hangers-on. They were butchered. We chased them right round the back of the station. Not everyone's a fast runner, and you could soon see which ones weren't up to the effort and were dropping off. I could hear a scouser whimpering in fear as he ran. A haymaker from the side wobbled him. Then he got tripped and you could feel the fear as he dropped, as did a few others. They got trampled and kicked a bit, but it was nothing compared to what would have happened to Mancs in the same position in Liverpool.

The police got things under control and pushed us all the way to the back of the Arndale. We were still revved up, but given the circumstances, a lot of lads threw the towel in and went for a late drink. There were now that many coppers that the Scousers would have to want it as much as us for anything to occur, and they patently didn't. The chat turned to how pathetic they were. They came to Manchester on the specials. The only time we'd seen them properly was at the station and at the ground. They'd not gone for a wander. At least in Liverpool they'd had a proper go.

Before we settled down to another beer, someone proposed one last look round the station and about twenty of us went back towards the Ducie Bridge. We did a left heading for the back of Victoria and what did we bump into but a similar number of Scousers. They knew who we were, we knew who they were, so there was no need for any chat. One of the lads with us was straight in and the rest of us flew in. We had with them in the middle of the road, and I have to say they were game. We had even numbers, but in our favour we had a proper knockout merchant from Salford. They didn't. He dropped three or four, which is always a wobbler because someone's got to take him on, and none of them fancied it. They ran. We chased those still on their feet back into the station. They made the sanctuary of Victoria and we weren't going to follow and take on half of GMP on our own.

On the way back we ran into these four who've picked themselves up. We could have been out of order and given them another slap, and they went to veer round.

'You've had yours, you won't be getting it again. You stood your ground so you're getting left.'

'We stood there to have a go, just to let you know that some of us will. I'll tell you straight it's been a pisspoor show us not coming on the service or anything. It's looked shite. We've had a slap and we'll take it, that's fair enough.'

With that we went our ways, them to the station, us for a drink. One lad had it right though. 'Wouldn't you fucking know it? Eleven pm at night before you meet any mickeys who want a proper bash.'

* * *

IN 1985, WE had a chance to stop Everton going for a Treble when we played them in the FA Cup final. That day there were many Scousers and Mancs at Wembley without tickets, but I think they all got in. Every little turrethole, turnstile, service gate and door was used.

Before the game, United swamped London; there were so many we were like an occupying force. It was unreal. The only bit of trouble I had was Friday night in Leicester Square when I got carted off to the cop shop. I was in a boozer dancing on the windowsill, pissed like everyone else, having been at it since 11am. I fell over, grabbed the curtain and pulled it off. Unfortunately the Old Bill were looking in through the window at the time. Anyway, things happened in the pub, the till and the fruit machine went west, and it was time to vacate. I thought no more if it, staggered out, and was arrested and put in the back of a van. They let me out a couple of hours later.

We were staying at a B&B in Kings Cross. At about 5.30am I found myself walking round to Euston where loads of United were dossing down. And at that unearthly hour, I had a fight with twenty Everton fans, their night-time jibbers. I was at the bottom of the stairs outside Euston, throwing punches and kicks, and people were jumping awake and running to join in. Eventually forty of us chased these Scousers to Kings Cross.

That day, however, is remembered by United not for the trouble or the result, but for the major jewellery snatch at Swiss Cottage.

Little Dessie: *In 1983 we had met at Swiss Cottage before the FA Cup final against Brighton. Wythenshawe, Salford and Collyhurst were all there and we had a belting day. The year after, Everton were in the final against Watford and they went to Swiss Cottage. So 1985, what happens? We get Everton in the FA Cup final. Now who is having Swiss Cottage?*

We get there in force, come out of the underground and it is full of Everton. They have got the pub and with it the ammo – bottles, beer glasses and stools. But after the first volley we are into them and chase them right down the high road. There is chaos on that road. The coppers cannot handle it.

An Asian guy comes out of his jewellery shop to watch us chase Everton down the road. Suddenly our mob stops. You could see the Scousers turning around, wondering why we had stopped chasing them. Well, what would you rather do, chase Scousers all day or rob a jewellery store? Everyone went in and grabbed whatever they could. The fellow couldn't do anything. Then you had loads of lads who, having earned their money for the day, were off in the slips. No-one is going to put themselves on offer when they've got a nice parcel of tom. That was a great result.

Thieving was a massive part of the day for a lot of lads. First there, best dressed, we used to say, particularly on trips to Europe. The mob would arrive in a city and then they'd all be off, in small groups, doing their thing. That was as much a part of it as the fighting. When I was a kid I begged my dad to take me to Old Trafford. He took me to the Stretford End and threw me in over the turnstiles. I was jibbing it and I didn't even know, but it set me on my path.

As I've said before I was never into thieving. I was no good at it. In the winter I was hod-carrying and in the summer I started working pop concerts, travelling around with all the grafters from Manchester. We went all over Europe selling tee-shirts.

The idea was to earn money but it always turned into a laugh and lots of time spent in boozers. The times I actually came home with money were few and far between.

We got up to all sorts. Elton John was one of the best tours. No-one fancied doing it so me and this other kid stepped in and were the only ones there. We smashed it. I did Michael Jackson the first time he went to Italy; ten of us played football on the Vatican steps and got chased off. One thing I discovered was that Manchester had easily the biggest firm grafting, both in this country and abroad. We would bump into the Scousers occasionally but a lot of the Manc grafters knew the Scouse grafters and people made sure that I didn't get involved with them, knowing my history with them at the football.

We did sometimes fight the stewards, especially in Germany. They would slap people and take their gear off them, then we would get to hear about it and when the concert was over we'd seek them out for some payback. We had some handy lads and were properly organised. We sold copies of the genuine merchandise and it was massive business. I have seen 400 grafters at Wembley.

I did the Madonna concerts there and reckoned I wouldn't sell many tee-shirts with all the competition. Instead I went to the landlord of the Torch pub and got a bin off him, which he filled with ice. Then I went to Tesco and bought loads of cans of booze. For four days I sat outside his pub with this bin, from early morning to late at night, knocking out cans. The landlord didn't care because his pub was rammed anyway. After the gig had finished all the grafters would come back to the Torch to count their money and divvy up and they were my best customers. I was back and forth to that supermarket in my van and made a killing.

The only time I saw trouble between grafters was when a firm of black lads from Birmingham turned up at Wembley. I spoke to a couple of them and they were a very handy bunch of lads, into martial arts. Usually, because of the criminal nature of what we were doing, any disputes got sorted out behind the scenes without much mither, but this lot were on Wembley Way when some Cockneys tried to do a couple of them. The black lads were well outnumbered but they gave it to the Cockneys, no messing.

There are only two main lads from other clubs I have ever got to know and that was through doing the concerts. One was a lad called Riley from Leeds, of all places, who I met at a Madonna concert. He is sound as a pound. The other was Hicky from Chelsea. He's alright, loud, a typical southerner. He knows he's not hard but he's part of a mob that loves to organise. I just wish once or twice they'd organised to come into Manchester.

Eventually the grafting game died away but while it lasted it took me all over Europe. It was always a top laugh, hiding on minibuses, sneaking onto boats. It did me good to get away. My wife Debbie thought about it the same as everything I did: she pulled her hair out.

CHAPTER FOURTEEN

THEY THINK IT'S ALL OVER

IT WAS ON a mad night out that I got the nickname many lads know me by today. We had come into town after a derby against City and occupied a two-storey boozer in one of the back streets behind Piccadilly. One lad knew the landlord and made some sort of deal to take us back to this pub because he was on an earner out of it. He knew how much we'd drink. All we were bothered about was that it was a decent meeting place to get together, have a few drinks and then head off for the inevitable attacks on City in town later that night.

The landlord said to me, 'Will you do the bar upstairs, Tony? The draught beer's off, so just give them cans, a pound apiece.' Then he slung a load of cases of cans up the stairs to me.

I stood behind the bar and starting doing these cans to the lads for a quid each. Then I thought, what the fuck am I doing behind a bar taking money off people for beer? I pulled the lever on the cider keg and discovered it was on. Fuck the cans: it was party time. I started filling pint pots with cider but couldn't serve the lads quick enough, so I got this big silver bucket from under the bar, pulled all the taps on and filled it continuously for people to top up out of. Others were filling up pint pots with spirits from the optics. Soon it was like watching a shoal of piranhas in a feeding frenzy. The downstairs emptied as word spread, 'O'Neill's giving the beer away.' There was nothing the landlord could do.

By the time the ale ran out, I was completely bladdered but still thinking I had to do the decent thing. I counted out £90 I'd received and gave the landlord £45. But his the place was in uproar. The fire extinguishers went off at me behind the bar. I ended up singing with this bucket on my head to protect me because they were all lobbing things at me: extinguishers, beer, ashtrays, beer trays, everything coming at me from 250 people smashed out of their heads.

Then we were out into the street, a bizarre sight at 10pm. The whole of town heard us singing, 'Where are the City fans?' We got to the Crown and Kettle pub in Ancoats and someone decided City were in there. I don't know if they were or not but everyone attacked the pub. They managed to lock the door but I stuck my head through the window and yelled that old terrace favourite, 'You're going to get you're fucking heads kicked in.' The police were waiting for us at the bottom of Oldham Street, which I suppose was just as well, as we were capable of anything that night.

And from then on I was Buckethead.

* * *

I HAVE HUNDREDS of tales of derby days but the story of the attack on the Whalley pub perhaps typifies them all. The first thing about a derby day is always, where are City meeting? That is the problem we have had every time, because they are so slippery. They are frightened of us turning up and pouncing on them. In all the time I was going to football, not once did they call it on with us before a game. They never said, 'We are meeting here, where are you meeting, we'll come and get you.'

They always kept schtum. We'd end up running around Fallowfield or wherever, trying to find them, and they'd be hiding. Everyone knows where we meet but City never come to attack us there. They want to pick people off on their own.

This day we were playing at Old Trafford and we knew that at some point they would make a show. The idea was to anticipate them. We met in a boozer we had never been in before or since, on an estate somewhere between the Whalley pub, on the edge of Whalley Range, and Chester Road. Four hundred of us were in there at 10am with the idea of catching them at some point as they came through the edge of Hulme or Moss Side.

City had actually met somewhere near Maine Road. We had people out looking but couldn't find them. Without us knowing it, they made their move and walked through to the Whalley. Completely by chance, we were in this pub just two streets away. We couldn't have planned it better.

Eventually we got the call that their firm had come across the park and were at the Whalley. There were no police about, both mobs were undetected. Perfect. We had them at last. Out we went, down the street and around the pub. There were some outside keeping guard but they must have been the worst guards in the world; as we came around the corner we were on them and they ran straight into the pub with barely time to warn anyone of our arrival. We swarmed around the pub and tried to kick in the door as they held it shut. The windows went in and everyone was shouting and beckoning them to come out.

We stepped back onto the pavement and they opened the door, making as though they were going to be brave. As they came out into the doorway we stormed forward again. The City at the front could not get back in because of the heroes at the back pushing them. Some were trying to throw chairs and glasses over the top at us.

At one point I had a chair and was in the middle of the doorway about to slam it on some lad's head when I recognised

235

him. But I was already halfway through my swing and so he copped it. What can you do? That's the nature of the game; it wasn't personal.

The City at the front got battered but all managed to get back inside. Then a kid came out wielding a blade. It looked like he'd come out to clear us back so the rest of them could follow. We encircled him, dancing around trying to grab his knife arm. He took a few whacks in the head and then got well done in, and I have to say none of them helped him.

At this point a police car screamed round the corner and pulled up. It got trashed. The driver had no choice but to reverse what was left of his vehicle and drive off again. We knew reinforcements would arrive soon and eventually the vans turned up. By then our job was done, so we charged off down the street with the cops behind us. City finally came out, a couple of hundred of them. They were a sorry sight.

We headed towards Old Trafford and loitered along the route, waiting for the police to escort them past. Some of them looked pretty bloodied and, as normal in those days, when they got to the corner of Warwick Road everyone joined in pelting them with cans and bottles and trying to pick them off. They were well and truly done that day. By staking out a nondescript pub on a nondescript estate, we had caught them hook, line and sinker.

Like I say, City like to pick you off when the odds are in their favour, and this did happen even to me one night in the Cyprus Tavern, a little town-centre club they liked to use at one time. I went in there with Little Des and eight of our younger lads after coming back from Derby. City had played at home and it was their club so lots of them were in there. Obviously it was moody but Des and I were full of it and no-one had a go – but the cunts kept one eye on us because we were getting more and more pissed.

At the end of the night we came to go up the stairs out into the street, absolutely full of keg, and the doorman warned, 'Look, they are all up there waiting for you.'

'Fuck 'em, let's go. Where are they?'

The young kids were flapping a bit because they knew the odds but Des and I were going up and they had to follow. As soon as we stepped out of the door, City came round the corner, arms outstretched in the fighting pose, bouncing on their toes.

'Come on!'

We went into them and a gap opened. A bottle whizzed past my ear and shattered behind me. Then they swarmed around. I tried to fight them off but I was too drunk and there were too many. I went over the bonnet of a car, still fighting and frankly amazed I was still there. I bounced off and then had no choice but to run with the younger lads. I started laughing at how ridiculous it was. The young kids weren't happy because they were being legged by City, but in truth we never had a chance in the first place. Des and I were happy we were still on our feet but they felt humiliated.

I got them across Oxford Road, keeping City in sight behind us. We whipped round a corner and I told them to stop because I knew the cunts running after us would be spread out by now – some always run faster than others. There was a beer crate there and I told them to get the bottles.

The first silly cunt comes round the corner. Smash, in his face and down he goes. The young ones are now happy. We give it to two or three of them. The first one is down, the second one is taking punches, the third one is getting it, but I know more are coming.

'Come on,' I said. We emptied the crate at the rest of them, then headed off down towards the universities. I hailed a cab, put a few of the young lads in it and told them to get off. Then Des and I made our own way home.

Some of the City who had attacked us were from Wythenshawe, but I don't take it personally. Whatever happens,

happens. I have had loads of fights like that and the next day you shrug it off. If you can't you shouldn't get involved.

* * *

BY THE MIDDLE of the Eighties, Maggie Thatcher had ordered the biggest ever crackdown against the hooligan firms. The horrors of Heysel and the Bradford fire, the death of a Leeds fan during a riot at Birmingham and our fight on the ferry with West Ham were the writing on the wall for many. Out of the blue, Hicky and his Chelsea firm were arrested after a lengthy undercover operation. Bill Gardner, Cass Pennant, Andy Swallow and their I.C.F. cronies also got a tug. Millwall were lifted. So were mobs from Oxford United, Leeds, Wolves, even Cambridge United.

Yet I wasn't stopping. This was the only life I knew. Chelsea away saw me back in my element, leading the firm to take on their mighty Headhunters. This time hundreds and hundreds of us came off the tube at Earls Court, wandered through some housing estate, and found ourselves on the Kings Road. This was what it was all about: in the heart of their territory, no coppers, game on.

Our chant whenever we ran into battle was, 'War.' We would start at a walk, and then as we got to the action the roar went and I tell you it was some frightening sound. By the time we reached the World's End, where Chelsea's pubs were, we were all running down the street bellowing. None of them could get out of their pubs as we went from one to the other, caning the windows. The Kings Road was ours.

Given the climate of the time, my exploits couldn't last, and in April 1986 I was nicked again, at Spurs. Our rivalry with them had, if anything, intensified after the tragedy at Seven Sisters tube station, and we had a big firm walking down Seven Sisters Road after the game. Tottenham came at us and there was loads of fighting, ebbing and flowing back and forth. When we got to the tube station, Tottenham tried to have a last go. I got stuck into them and we fought them off, but the coppers spotted me in the thick of it. I could see them pointing me out and now it was on top for me with London's finest.

Me and this kid Jason got offside, moving away from the main firm. The coppers took everyone down into the tube station and we stood on the platform, giggling because we'd had a row. We got on the train and it was then I noticed these coppers stood next to me. I sensed something was wrong, so I sat down away from the lads, as if I wasn't with them, and ignored any attempts at conversation. But the cops clearly had their eyes on me, and the next thing, they jumped on me and dragged me off.

Sat next to me in the nick was Jimmy O'Neill, no relation, a London kid and a top lad. Now when the cops asked who I was, I gave my brother's name, which was also Jimmy O'Neill. I was hoping to sow a bit of confusion and perhaps get off with it – until a lad called Nev Pitt, an out-and-out thief off our estate, came flying into the station, bladdered, and started shouting, 'Alright Tony, what are you doing here?' I give him the stare to tell him to shut his mouth, and eventually I got bailed – as Jimmy O'Neill.

When I returned for my trial, I got a court-appointed solicitor, a right tosser who clearly didn't believe a word I said – although to be fair, I was lying anyway. In court the cops said I had been fighting all the way up Seven Sisters and leading the mob, but there were a few discrepancies in their story. They tried to make out that they chased me down the tube steps, which was not true; they had waited until it had calmed down before arresting me.

As I stood in the dock, they produced this big file of previous convictions for Jimmy O'Neill; they had given me the sheet from the London kid who'd been next to me in the nick. It was paper after paper of GBH and God knows what. I told the court that I was *Tony* O'Neill and they had got it all wrong. Obviously I hoped the mix-up might get me off, making out that the police had got my name wrong in the nick and had confused me with this other lad. The copper knew I was lying, I knew I was lying, my solicitor knew I was lying and the court knew I was lying, and the only reason I half got away with it was because there had indeed been a James O'Neill arrested at the same time. But I was never going to win my case. The main cop told his lies, I told mine and the magistrates were that pissed off with me that they decided in thirty seconds they preferred the police lies to mine and sent me to jail for four months. The newspapers called me 'a notorious football hooligan and businessman.'

They stuck me in Pentonville. It was the dirtiest, smelliest jail you could ever have the misfortune to go in. It was full of down and outs, tramps, non-payers of fines. I slept in a cell with blankets that tramps had had. There was no such thing as laundry. No-one said boo to me; I was known simply as 'the Manc'. It was the most horrible place you could ever spend a vacation.

Two days after I had been banged up, the West Ham ferry incident was all over the news. I suppose it was a good thing that I was doing my four months; I would have been on that boat and I'd have got ten years. The fight would certainly have been different.

* * *

WHILE I WAS in jail, the so-called football intelligence police in Manchester started sending me letters saying I had to report to Stockport police station on certain days at 5.30pm when England were playing – and if I didn't turn up they were going to arrest me. My missus wrote back sarcastically asking if it would be possible to get me a day release from prison to attend to sign on – 'But my husband was also wanting to know is it possible could you send him a form for loss of earnings, as he earns £1.40 a day where he is. And is there a scheme where you can sort out a railway warrant for him, as he would like to turn up because he wouldn't want to be arrested, as it is your football intelligence that put him in prison in the first place.' They didn't even know I was in prison. Brilliant.

The same copper who nicked me came up to me ten years later at Wembley when we played Chelsea in the FA Cup final.

'Alright Tony?' he said. 'How are you?'

'I'm alright. Who are you?'

'I nicked you at Tottenham.'

'You fucking cunt. The one who got me sent down and you lied through your teeth, you wanker.'

He winked at me and walked off. But that showed they were still watching me.

When I came out, even I could see the writing on the wall. The cops at Manchester were happy to boast that Old Trafford was now one of the best policed and most secure grounds in the country. The Chief Superintendent, Arthur Roberts, claimed that Old Trafford was in many ways used as a model for the recommendations which came out of the Popplewell Report in the wake of Heysel, Birmingham and Bradford City. They had installed a range of surveillance cameras around the ground and its approaches, feeding back to a control room. These were not just to stop trouble but for intelligence gathering. The government had banned the sale of alcohol at football grounds, except in restaurants and similar areas. There was widespread discussion of identity cards around this time, though in the end they were never introduced. They had also brought a Home Office 'hoolivan' to Old Trafford, for mobile crowd observation.

The media had also tired of the exploits of hooligans. In Manchester, where the papers had devoted acres of newsprint to the exploits of the Red Army in the Seventies, reporters were becoming preoccupied with the city's gang war. Shootings had started in Moss Side and Salford, and criminals were fighting for control of nightclub doors and the drugs trade, which was big business. The Hacienda was about to have its heyday, and ecstasy was on the way. I suppose blokes running around punching each other on the streets seemed tame by comparison.

Unbeknown to me, the police in Manchester had not given up though. They had formed an undercover group called the Omega Squad, and their intention was to infiltrate the hooligans of Manchester United and Manchester City and collect evidence that we were conspiring to cause violent disorder at football grounds. They had a list of those they most wanted, and one man above all was their main target; the man they called the 'prime mover'. He was given a special codename: Target Kilo.

You can probably guess his identity. But that's another story . . .

Coming soon from Milo Books

The Sequel to *Red Army General*:

THE MEN IN BLACK
Leading Manchester United's Hooligan Firm, 1988–2001

Tony O'Neill

Including:

- Operation Mars: the police probe into Manchester United's hooligans, and how it fell apart

- West Ham away: the Night of the Balaclavas

- Leeds United: the Wheatsheaf Battles, no police, just two mobs

- The Treble: travels in our greatest ever season

- Boxing clever: trouncing the Zulus at the NEC

- The Birth of the Men In Black: Aldgate East (West Ham again)

- The Truth about Beckham: Budapest Airport

- Cardiff: the Soul Crew get a shock at Poet's Corner

- Liverpool: infiltrating the Main Stand

- Newcastle: having it in the street with the Gremlins

- Glasgow Rangers away: the unbeatable 500

- Jailed: how I was sent down for football hooliganism for the final time

- And much, much more